D0317460

Mary Ann Cotton
– Dark Angel

Previous Publications

e Potted History of West Auckland

The Miners' Triumph –
The First English World Cup Win in Football History

Mary Ann Cotton
– Dark Angel

Britain's First Female Serial Killer

Martin Connolly

EAST AYRSHIRE LEISURE TRUST	
532764	
Bertrams	16/09/2016
364.152	£14.99
	D T

First published in Great Britain in 2016 by
TRUE CRIME
an imprint of
Pen and Sword Books Ltd
47 Church Street
Barnsley
South Yorkshire S70 2AS

Copyright © Martin Connolly, 2016

ISBN 978 1 47387 620 0

The right of Martin Connolly to be identified
as the author of this work has been asserted by him in
accordance with the Copyright, Designs and Patents Act 1988.

A CIP record for this book is available from the British Library
All rights reserved. No part of this book may be reproduced or
transmitted in any form or by any means, electronic or
mechanical including photocopying, recording or
by any information storage and retrieval system, without
permission from the Publisher in writing.

Printed and bound in England
by CPI Group (UK) Ltd, Croydon, CR0 4YY

Typeset in Plantin by
CHIC GRAPHICS

Pen & Sword Books Ltd incorporates the imprints of
Pen & Sword Archaeology, Atlas, Aviation, Battleground, Discovery,
Family History, History, Maritime, Military, Naval, Politics, Railways,
Select, Social History, Transport, True Crime, Claymore Press,
Frontline Books, Leo Cooper, Praetorian Press, Remember When,
Seaforth Publishing and Wharncliffe.

For a complete list of Pen and Sword titles please contact
Pen and Sword Books Limited
47 Church Street, Barnsley, South Yorkshire, S70 2AS, England
E-mail: enquiries@pen-and-sword.co.uk
Website: www.pen-and-sword.co.uk

Contents

TRIAL, SENTENCE, & CONDEMNATION
OF
MARY ANN COTTON,
THE WEST AUCKLAND SECRET POISONER,

Who is under "Sentence of Death" for the murder of Her Husband, Children and other Persons by poison, so that she might get their Funeral Money.

Tune:- Driven From Home.

The West Auckland Poisoner, at last had been tried,
That she is guilty cannot be denied,
Her crimes have struck terror all over the land,
And deep indignation on every hand.
No feelings of pity was in her hard heart,
She never has acted the good woman's part;
With dark deeds of murder she perill'd her soul,
And her children destroyed for possessions of gold.

CHORUS

No one can pity, no one can bless,
Mary Ann Cotton for her wickedness;
The West Auckland poisoner condemned doth lie,
She murdered her children, and soon she must die.

Her poor little children' dear lives she betrayed,
For the sake of the money the burial clubs paid;
She stood by and saw them struggling with pain,
Her crime she repeated again and again.
The poison she gave them when no one was nigh,
And in fearful agony each one did die;
Altho' in bad deeds her life has been past,
The judgement of Heav'in has reached her at last.

For months this bad woman in a prison was hurled,
Till another poor offspring she brought in the world.
Born in a prison amidst crime and shame,
With an unfeeling mother unworthy the name.
How happy it is that seldom we hear,
Of women poisoning their children so dear;
In this world below, or the bright world above.
A heavenly gift is a true mother's love

She murdered her husbands and a lodger as well,
The numbers she poisoned no one can tell.
So anxious she was for the money they said,
That she ordered the coffins before they were dead.
The strong hand of justice compell'd her to stay,
And her crimes have been proved as clear as the day.
Now in Durham prison condemn'd she does lie,
And soon on the scaffold she will have to die.

The man or the woman who God now offends,
And by secret poison encompass their ends,
From the strong hardy man to the infant at birth,
No one is safe while they stay on the earth.
When murder is committed in a moment of rage,
We often can pity and petition to save.
But Mary Ann Cotton who in Durham doth lie,
Every-one knows she's deserving to die.

Oh what must she think as she lays in her cell,
The day and the hour of her death she can tell.
Her heart must be harder than iron or stone;
If she don't repent for the crimes she has done.
No blessing she'll have.no sympathy get,
No one will pity, none will regret;
It is only justice most people will cry,
When Mary Ann Cotton shall stand up to die.

London — H P SUCH, Machine Printer,

and publisher, 177, Union Street, Borough

A song sheet that was for sale on the streets of Victorian England immediately after Mary Ann Cotton's trial, which shows the hysteria and prejudice of the time.

The Writing of this Story

Over the years, as I have stood in my Sub-Post office at West Auckland, I have had many visitors to the village who pop in to ask questions about the village's history and people. As a response I wrote the booklet *The Potted History of West Auckland*. It was well received and as a consequence I have been asked, by many of those who have read it, to write further on one of the topics: Mary Ann Cotton. The last house in which Mary Ann Cotton lived sits diagonally opposite my office, on the other side of the large village green. Daily I looked at the house and considered the requests to write something on her. Over the years in my various careers, I had carried out research in a number of areas, and decided to see if there was anything worth researching with Mary Ann Cotton. For the *Potted History*, I had relied on internet research only and repeated the simple facts and myths that were there. I therefore decided to ignore the modern reports on the internet and go right back to the time of Mary Ann Cotton, to look at the primary sources for the events. The records of The National Archives and the Durham Records Office were great sources of material. The libraries of Durham and Sunderland proved excellent resources. I read, I believe, every newspaper account of the life and times of Mary Ann, in newspapers from all over the UK, including those in Guernsey. I discovered her case had been quite a cause célèbre.

In a sense I began to 'live' in the 1800s with Mary Ann and those around her. I noticed that Mary Ann was the centre of everything, with the focus on her alone. This, of course, is understandable, but those around her had lives too and deserved their own voices to be heard. It was this that guided me to try and ensure they too would be given notice, as much as possible, in what I would decide to produce. When I had brought together all my material and thoughts, I then turned to see what books on Mary Ann Cotton were being recommended. In this, two stood out, *Mary Ann Cotton – Her Story and Trial* by Arthur Appleton and *Mary Ann*

Cotton Dead, But Not Forgotten by Tony Whitehead. Arthur's account has some factual and date errors, but was a good read. It was on reading Tony Whitehead's book that I had a moment of wishing I had started with that particular book. In it, he had amassed a large number of images of birth, death and baptismal records. It would have saved me a great deal of time, energy and money. However, in one way, I was also happy that I had done it the way I had, because it allowed me to use Tony Whitehead's book to confirm a lot of my findings and details. It also helped me abandon a number of ideas I was considering and to expand on others. As a result of reading these books, I decided the story needed attention and a new neutral approach. I also wanted to further develop areas involving those around Mary Ann, and hoped to give an updated comment on the Mary Ann Cotton story.

My final act of research was to travel around the sites of Mary Ann Cotton's life, to try and strip away the modern façade and to get a feel for how she and her contemporaries lived. Seaham, Pallion, Bishop-wearmouth, South Hetton, and the pit villages around the area, brought home the narrowness of the world in which Mary Ann Cotton lived. In some places there still survive relics of the time that brought home the harshness and difficulties of her existence. Seeing how the large city of Newcastle contrasted with the small pit village of Easington Lane, for example, was useful in exploring Mary Ann's mind-set; of the girl from a little village having her eyes opened by the grandness of the city. It was a helpful experience to explore the cemeteries and churches involved in the story and to imagine the scenes of the various lives that had ended and whose remains were placed in these grounds.

I already knew my own village well and its smallness, in many ways, made clear the very common and open background to what happened in this village where Mary Ann Cotton was first exposed. To stand in the graveyard at St Helen Auckland Parish Church and consider it being almost entirely dug up in the search for evidence, all added a sense of the drama that unfolded in the late nineteenth century.

The first work has been expanded and fresh material added in response to a greater interest in the story. I therefore relate here my understanding of that tale and trust that it will help give insight into Mary Ann Cotton and those around her, and perhaps even challenge the myths that have surrounded her.

I would also like to thank the staff at The National Archives and of the Durham Records Office, who were excellent in their help, time and advice. Thanks to my family, especially my wife, Kitty, and my daughter, Esther, who were very much involved in helping my research and Angela, my step-daughter, in listening to my thoughts and ideas and offering criticism.

Introduction

Standing at modern Bondgate in Bishop Auckland, where the old police station and courts have long gone, and seeing shoppers, school children, businessmen and mothers dragging obstinate children, the scene is far removed from August 1872. Here on this street, Mary Ann Cotton was brought to spend a few days in a spartan police station cell. In those days the place was dark and foreboding. The bed on which Mary Ann would have lain was hard with a woollen cloth that was both mattress and blanket. Wednesday, 21 August 1872 would be a defining day for Mary Ann. She would walk upstairs to face two magistrates. They were the Reverend James W. Hick who was the Rector at Byers Green. He lived there with his wife, Jane, and family. The other was Dr John Jobson, a surgeon who lived close to the court at Market Square with his wife, Mary. He would have been a colleague and acquaintance of Dr Kilburn from nearby West Auckland who would be a key player in Mary Ann's trial.

We then take a long walk along Newgate, today a narrow street of shops and offices. It was along this street Mary Ann was walked by two police officers after her hearing. People who had been present in the court now preceded her, calling to others the outcome of the case. Mothers would pull their children close to them, as by now Mary Ann's reputation was used to frighten the 'bairns'. We arrive outside Bishop Auckland's railway station, much changed since its heyday, when four tracks passed through it. Now only one track carries local trains. It is surrounded by modern retail stores and banks. It is difficult to transport yourself back to 1872, when a crowd gathered to catch a glimpse of the West Auckland Borgia, so named by the papers. They would jeer and hiss at a woman heading for trial in Durham, but who had already been found guilty in the court of public opinion.

We now begin our story of this woman, which we find centred on the coal mines of County Durham

Chapter 1

The Beginnings

County Durham lies in the North East of England; an area dominated by its ecclesiastical knight-bishops and coal mining. Fiercely independent, it would not submit itself to the rule of Northumberland which claimed it. In 1293, it snubbed the justices of Northumberland and appealed to parliament for its separation from their rule. This stubborn and independent spirit bred men and women who were hardy and resourceful, and to whom violence and death were no strangers. The tough character of this area's people would be needed as coal was

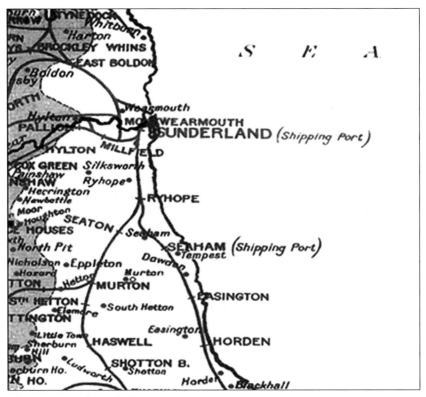

The pits around South Hetton.

discovered and mines were sunk throughout its territory. With the mines came danger, ill-health and poverty alongside the contrasts of strict Christianity and heavy alcoholism. It was here that many men tried to raise families in conditions that were harsh, facing constant battles for better pay and conditions from the mine owners. The practice of being bound to an owner for a year on meagre wages was a source of great anger and frustration – anger that would boil over into violence. Often the police and soldiers would be called out to keep the peace. A typical report in the local paper in 1831 shows the tensions involved. Indeed in 1832 one of the biggest strikes ever to hit the North East caused great division and concern.

THE PITMAN of THE TYNE and WEAR

We are glad to learn that all the pits In the Lambton Colliery and also those of the Marquis of Londonderry have at length resumed working, of course with bound men. In the other collieries, however, the difference between the coal-owners and the pitmen remain unadjusted, and with but little prospect of immediate settlement, as the conduct of the latter from its fickle and unreasonable character, is found to interpose an insurmountable barrier to a satisfactory arrangement.

One claim conceded, another started, and so on without end. Meanwhile, the system of begging, intimidation, and violence, which we so often had occasion to condemn, continues to be practised in all its terrors, and with such injurious consequences, both to misguided men themselves and to the public that we feel justified in calling upon the magistracy to repress it by the exercise of the ample powers with which they are invested. The coal-owners, in order to provide habitations for workmen who are willing to serve them, are beginning to use force in ejecting the refractory pitmen from their houses: and no less vigour and determination is manifested by them for the preservation of the peace, and the restoration of order, in other respects. Six men were, on Thursday, committed to our jail, for trial at the next sessions, on a charge of rioting at Lambton, and ten others to hard labour for three months for threatening the bound workmen

employed by Lord Durham, and preventing them from going to work. The prisoners were escorted to the jail by a party of dragoons. At the beginning of the week, a formidable disturbance took place at Hetton, when Mr. Wood the cashier of the colliery, was maltreated in endeavouring to protect a man whom the mob were about to strip and beat. The military, we understand had to be called in to quell the tumult; and it was only by the aid of a party of soldiers that the two ringleaders could be subsequently taken into custody.
Durham Chronicle

The matter was raised in a letter to *The Times*:

Dated Durham, April 24, 9 p.m.:— I am anxious to inform you, that a foul and deliberate murder was committed at Hetton last Saturday night, by some of the unbound men, who basely way-laid and shot a man who was bound. I am glad to say we have got a clue to the perpetrators of the horrid deed, and have little doubt of being able to bring the charge home to the right persons. Several are implicated. Ten men were sent to gaol last night for further examination. The Governor has been at Hetton to-day, with one of them, and is to return to-morrow, under an escort of dragoons. The coroner's inquest is still sitting, and will be adjourned over to-night. Magistrates, military, the committee, London police, &c., are daily and nightly at Hetton; of course no work is going on at the pits, but proper measures are taken for securing a sufficient number of lead miners, and I hope it will not be long ere we succeed in resuming our labours. We have turned out several families and that unpleasant though necessary work will go on progressively. Notwithstanding all the differences, Hetton itself and the neighbourhood is perfectly quiet to all appearance. The fact is, the pitmen are overawed by superior force, or, there is no doubt, they would be in a state of riot and open rebellion. They even submit to turn out, and have all their goods put into the street, without uttering a murmur; indeed many of them consider it a kind of triumph.

MARY ANN COTTON – DARK ANGEL

The article and letter demonstrates the ruthlessness under which miners had to work. Their jobs, homes and families were at the mercy of men who wanted to make their fortunes in coal. It is hard for modern minds to imagine conditions in mining at this time. Wages were low. Men had to buy certain items needed for the job out of this poor income. Health and safety was never considered to any great degree. Bad air, the risk of flooding and explosion and the fear of a collapse was the lot of a miner. This then was the background to the life of Mary Ann Cotton, who became notorious as the West Auckland Poisoner.

It was 1812, in the reign of King George III, of madness fame. The United States of America declared war on Britain, and Napoleon was invading Russia. John Bellingham assassinated the prime minister, Spencer Perceval, in the lobby of the House of Commons in London. In the North of England, at Jarrow, a mine explosion at Felling colliery killed ninety-six miners. It was into this world that Michael Robson was born in South Hetton, a village that had grown up around the mining industry. Pits were established there and at Haswell, Murton and Easington, amongst others. It had a railway built between it and Seaham Harbour in

The modern St Michael and All Angels.

1833. Mining was everything to the area, indeed it was the centre of life for the population. Michael Robson was born into a mining family.

Michael was taken to the church of St Michael and All Angels to be baptised on 27 September 1812. The following year Margaret Lonsdale was born in the village of Tanfield, in County Durham. Margaret was taken to St Margaret's Church on 25 July 1813 to be baptised. These two would be forever linked to notoriety as the parents of Mary Ann Cotton.

Back in Durham, in 1832, cholera was rampant throughout the area and many were dying as it swept across the South Hetton district. In the North East of England, 31,000 people died of the disease in 1832 alone. Life was miserable, work was dangerous and the hard winter brought heavy snow and ice. Deaths of both adults and children were commonplace and gastric flu could easily disguise the effects of poisoning, providing a backdrop to the many deaths that would accompany Mary Ann Cotton.

Michael Robson, only just turned twenty, sought comfort from the rigors of his life in the arms of 19-year-old Margaret Lonsdale. The two allowed passion to rule and the comfort Margaret gave led to an urgent need to get married. Margaret announced to Michael the news that she was expecting a child. He would have taken the news with stoicism. Despite their situation, both were from a solid Methodist background, and they lived their lives with the strong work ethic of their faith, accepting whatever God sent their way. Indeed they may have viewed the pregnancy as God's way to force them into making their relationship 'honest'. They married in July 1832.

On 31 October that year Margaret was delivered of a baby girl who, as custom demanded, was presented for baptism at St Mary's Church, West Rainton, on 11 November 1832.

Mary Ann Robson's birth entry.

As the Reverend Tiffin, the local curate, intoned the usual blessing and then poured the water onto the baby's head, he spoke the name that the parents had chosen for their first born, Mary Ann.

Mary Ann Robson's baptism entry.

Thus, Mary Ann Robson was officially welcomed into the Christian community. She would grow in her Methodist faith mainly under the instruction of her mother, but her father would also insist on a strict observation of the rules and rites associated with the Methodist faith. At the time of her trial, a Wesleyan minister who knew her made this report in the *Northern Echo*:

> Mr Holdforth, who is now a class-leader in connection with the Wesleyan body in West Hartlepool, made his acquaintance with the condemned woman upwards of thirty years ago, when, as he describes her, she was a most exemplary and regular attender at a Wesleyan Sunday-school at Murton village, of which he occasionally officiated as the superintendent. At that time, it seems, she was regarded as a girl of innocent disposition and average intelligence. Michael Robson, her father, who was a sinker at Murton Colliery, was much respected in the neighbourhood and saw that his daughter received as good an education as was obtainable at the village school. Such was her general behaviour that she soon managed to win the good opinion of all who knew her, and she was distinguished for her particularly clean and tidy appearance.

This testimony is in stark contrast to the Mary Ann Cotton of modern repute. At this time of her life we find an intelligent and well-presented young girl, well thought of in her community.

In the village of Murton, Mary Ann was introduced to the local Methodist circuit as she grew up and, in early adolescence, took on the role of Sunday school teacher to the local younger children of Methodist parents. As we have seen from Mr Holdforth above, no one in those early days would have had any idea of what lay ahead for this young, pretty black-haired lass.

Meanwhile, Michael Robson eked out a living in the coalfields where his was the dangerous job of sinking shafts in the new mines that were being discovered. The Robson family moved into East Rainton where Michael found work at the Hazard Pit. Margaret was pregnant again and on 28 July 1834 another girl was born and given the same name as her mother. The young Margaret lived only a matter of months, her death caused by one of the many illnesses that afflicted the poor. The family moved to the North Hetton colliery and then made a further move to the East Murton colliery in 1835. It was in that year his wife announced she was carrying another child. Mary Ann became a sister to the new arrival, Robert, who was born on 5 October 1835. Mary Ann welcomed her brother, Robert, into the family when she was 3 years old. From then on she would have to learn to share the meagre resources of this poor family. Perhaps the seeds of wanting betterment, money and goods were sown in

1841 Census, Michael Robson and family.

the soil of this poverty and hardship. Did the young Mary Ann have to wear patched dresses and was it this that sowed in her the desire for fancy expensive dresses in later life?

The 1841 Census also shows the small Robson family, including the 5-year-old Robert, living in Durham Place at Murton.

By the time of the 1841 Census, Mary Ann was 8 years of age and her father, Michael, was still engaged in the dangerous work of sinking shafts at the Murton colliery for the South Hetton Coal Company. Mr Potter, the viewer engineer at the company, was triumphant in the success at the sinking of the pit.

South Hetton Mine Monument.

The following report appeared in the *Newcastle Journal*

THE SOUTH HETTON COLLIERY: The South Hetton Coal Company (Col. Bradyll and partners) have conquered all difficulty and succeeded in sinking through the sand at their extensive new winning of a colliery at Murton, near Dalton-le-Dale. This great achievement in the mining world was effected on Thursday, when great rejoicing took place among the workmen, by whose exertions and zeal, guided by the ability and energy of Mr Potter, the viewer and engineer, the great work was accomplished.

The report points to the danger of sinking shafts into difficult ground where shifting sands were a hazard. Indeed this success, as always in the coalfields in those days, was at a cost to human life. Six months after the report in the press of the success at Murton, Mary Ann's father would pay the price for this most celebrated event. He had been among those who had rejoiced and it was the exertion and zeal of men like him that brought the company its success. However, now 26 years of age, in February 1842, Michael Robson was again working in a shaft at the Murton Colliery. It was not a deep shaft, only 300ft. No doubt the difficult sandy conditions were not helpful, but whatever the cause, Michael Robson fell to his death and was crushed as the shaft gave way. The broken and shattered body of Michael was dragged out of the mine and was wrapped in a sack bearing the stamp 'Property Of The South Hetton Coal Company'. The body was delivered to his grieving widow, Margaret, on a small wooden coal-cart.

We can only imagine the scene as Mary Ann, with her arm around her younger brother, stood with their mother. The grief stricken Margaret is left shattered with the body of her husband. His death meant not only the loss of a beloved husband, but also of an income and a roof over her head. Michael's hard work, with its pitiful wages, ended in the ignominy of being brought home like a sack of coal; just one of many who would end their lives this way. Such was the lot of a hard working father and miner. Michael's Body was buried at West Rainton.

The tragedy was that in the coalfields, the loss of the miner in a tied cottage meant the widow and children would be evicted. However, Margaret, ever resourceful, had remarried within the year to George Stott, another miner. He was born at Gateshead in 1816. George was also a stout Methodist and he continued to raise the children as his own. Mary Ann, so recently losing her own father, did not take well to George.

Chapter 2

The Mowbrays

Mary Ann would have been raised a strict Methodist by both her own father and by George Stott. Her connections within the Methodist circuit and status as a Sunday school teacher would have instilled in her a sense of right and wrong. With such a background and the hand of a strict step-parent it is no wonder that at 16, when Mary Ann was given the opportunity, she left home. Her first post was as an under-nurse for Edward Potter, a manager working as a viewer in the South Hetton mines, who we have already met through the report in the local press. It is likely Potter was very sympathetic to Mary Ann, being aware of the loss of her father at his mine, and perhaps feeling partly responsible. The Potters lived well in the large South Hetton House and had a range of domestic help. In 1841 there were five children and six domestic servants living with Edward Potter and his wife, Margaret. Moving from a miner's cottage to such a grand house would be an eye-opener for Mary Ann. Here she would see what money could do. The intelligent Mary Ann would see that the Potters' success was built on the back of the miners who sweated and died in the pits. However, this would become the lifestyle that Mary Ann aspired to and her journey from here would always be in search of a husband who could deliver it.

The local newspapers, such as the Northern Echo, suggested the possibility that later on Margaret Cotton also had a position at South Hetton House because her career was that of domestic laundry servant. Mary Ann was hired to look after Potter's large family and as a young girl the experience must have been a challenge. From newspaper reports at the time of the trial, Mary Ann did a great job and Potter's wife spoke well of her. There was no trace of any harm to the children or those in Potter's household. It would appear that the Potter children were eventually dispersed into boarding schools around Darlington and so the

George Stott, 1851 Census.

post came to an end and she left the Potter home to return to her step-father's house. In the 1851 Census we find Margaret, George, Mary Ann and Robert all living at Murton Colliery. Mary Ann is now 18 years old.

Mary Ann did what was necessary in the poor conditions of the time and took another job, this time as an apprentice dressmaker, a job that would help her create the beautiful clothes she longed for. However, Mary Ann began to show a character trait that would be seen throughout the rest of her life. Although she was never described as beautiful, she was 'pleasant looking' or 'pretty' and it became clear she could attract men to marry her. So it was that she brought 26-year-old William Mowbray under her spell. He was born in Shotley, Northumberland. It was thought he had come up to the north of England from the Cambridgeshire cathedral city of Peterborough – although census information in 1861 would suggest he was born in Shotley. We do know he was hard at work on building sites around Shotley as a teenager. He was a travelling man who would go where the work took him, hiring himself out to contractors, so he may well have spent some time in Peterborough. We know from her later life that Mary Ann used her seductive powers to gain advantage and it is thought that she became pregnant by William. Local newspapers reported that he found himself standing at the altar of St Andrews Church in Newcastle where he took the young Mary Ann as his wife on 18 July 1852. However, records from the Newcastle Registry show they were in fact married there instead. It is possible that what happened at the church was a 'blessing', quite common for marriages that were deemed irregular. There would be no record of this type of event. The evidence of a non-Church wedding, for the Methodist Mary Ann, would confirm that this was a hurried marriage of convenience to legitimise the pregnancy. The marriage also reveals that Mary Ann was prepared to bend the truth, when she declares her age as 21, when in reality it was about 19, below the age of majority at that time.

There is much speculation at this point as to what happened next. The evidence of the jobs he took on suggests William was a decent man who worked hard for his family. What is known is that William and Mary Ann moved almost immediately away from South Hetton. The common belief is that they went straight to the south of England. In that day-and-age, and with Mary Ann's Methodist background, the couple would want to leave the area. William had spent a great deal of time in the south and it would be natural for him to head to a place he was familiar with. So they spent the next few years around the south, particularly in the Plymouth or Southampton area for a period. Reports at the time of Mary Ann's trial spoke of four or five children having come and gone whilst the Mowbray's were away from the north. It would probably be right to assume that all the deaths would have been certified as being caused by gastric fever or one of the many childhood illnesses very common throughout Victorian England at that time.

A search through the whole of England's registers for any evidence of births to the Mowbrays between 1852 and 1856, with approximately 150 registrations being examined, did not turn up a single record. It may well be that the couple lived a nomadic existence for a time and did not get round to making registrations of births and deaths. At that time such things were not regulated as they are today. What we do know is that Mary Ann became pregnant around September 1855 and the couple moved to St Germans in Cornwall where William took a job with the railway as a storekeeper. It was on 23 June 1856 that Mary Ann was delivered of a baby girl. They gave the new daughter the name Margaret Jane.

Just after the birth there was a softening in relationship between the Mowbrays and the Stotts. Mary Ann's mother visited the family in St Germans and the result was a move back to the north east of England. William and Mary Ann settled at Murton Colliery where William took on another storekeeping job. The baby Margaret Jane, born in St Germans, was brought to St Andrews in Dalton Le Dale on 5 April 1857 where the Rev J.H. Brown took her into the Church community. William left his job as storekeeper and began to work on ships out of Sunderland as a stoker

CERTIFIED COPY OF AN ENTRY OF BIRTH						GIVEN AT THE **GENERAL REGISTER OFFICE**			
						Application Number 4271952-2			

REGISTRATION DISTRICT				ST GERMANS					
1856 BIRTH in the Sub-district of St Germans				in the County of Cornwall					

Columns:-	1	2	3	4	5	6	7	8	9	10
No.	When and where born	Name, if any	Sex	Name and surname of father	Name, surname and maiden surname of mother	Occupation of father	Signature, description and residence of informant	When registered	Signature of registrar	Name entered after registration
438	Twenty third June 1856 St Germans	Margaret Jane	Girl	William Mowbray	Mary Ann Mowbray formerly Robson	Railway Storekeeper	Mary Ann Mowbray Mother St Germans	Ninth July 1856	Richard Polgreen Registrar	

CERTIFIED to be a true copy of an entry in the certified copy of a Register of Births in the District above mentioned.

Given at the GENERAL REGISTER OFFICE, under the Seal of the said Office, the 22nd day of August 2012

BXCF 532733

CAUTION: THERE ARE OFFENCES RELATING TO FALSIFYING OR ALTERING A CERTIFICATE AND USING OR POSSESSING A FALSE CERTIFICATE ©CROWN COPYRIGHT

WARNING: A CERTIFICATE IS NOT EVIDENCE OF IDENTITY.

IPS 045088 35933 10/10 3MSPSL 028231

Margaret Jane Mowbray born in Cornwall.

from 1858. William being busy at sea did not stop Mary Ann becoming pregnant in early 1858 and in December of that year Mary delivered another daughter, Isabella Jane, into the family.

She was presented for baptism at Holy Trinity on 19 December 1859, where the curate Rev Lazenby did the honours.

Sadly, Margaret Jane died in June 1860, aged 4. There was a great deal of confusion at the time of Mary Ann's trial about this child.

The name Mary Ann Mowbray was often quoted. This was due to an error on the parish burial register. It shows that the registrar of the records had inserted the mother's name in the deceased name's column.

In June 1861 we find that William Mowbray is registered as living at a pub in South Hetton, with Mary Ann and Isabella.

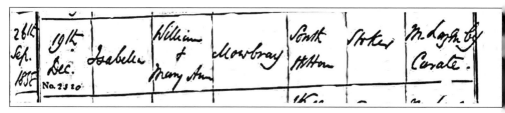

Isabella Mowbray baptism entry.

Holy Trinity Church, South Hetton.

Mary Jane Mowbray burial record.

24

214	Public House	1		William Mowbray	Head	Mar	35		Stoker	Northumberland Scotty
				Mary A. D°	Wife	Mar	28		D° Wife	Durham Houghtle-Spring
				Isabella D°	Daur		2			D° Hadington
215		1		George Stott	Head	Mar	44		Coal Miner	D° Gateshead
				Margaret D°	Wife	Mar	47		D° Wife	D° Tanfield
216		1		Thomas Wheatley	Head	Mar	79		Ag Labourer	D° Lanchester
				Hannah D°	Wife	Mar	71		D° Wife	D° Sedgefield
217		1		Ralph Chapman	Head	Mar	49		Boot & Shoemaker	D° Eddington
				Mary D°	Wife	Mar	49		D° Wife	D° Chester-le-St
				Ann D°	Daur	Un	20		Dress Maker	D° Eddington
	Total of Males and Females...						11	13		

Mowbrays and Stotts together at South Hetton, 1861 Census.

The Stotts are also living there. It is not possible to identify which pub it was, as there were a number of pubs in South Hetton at the time.

The Newburn was a boat built by James Laing in 1861 for Fenwick and Sons, and was a steam/sailing ship class, commissioned on 9 March 1861. The captaincy of the vessel was given to master mariner John Hubbard, originally from Barking in Essex; back in March 1839, John Hubbard had married Mary Ann's aunt, Jane Lonsdale, and he and Jane lived at Lawrence Street, Sunderland. It would appear that William Mowbray signed on as one of *The Newburn's* original crew, thanks to Mary Ann's uncle, John Hubbard. The census of 1861 confirms William Mowbray's occupation as a stoker.

The 1861 census also helps us keep track of Mary Ann who is pregnant again. On 2 October 1861, another daughter arrived, and was baptised Margaret Jane Mowbray at Holy Trinity by curate Lazenby, on 1 December 1861.

South Hetton, 2012.

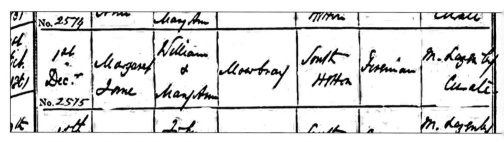

Margaret Jane Mowbray (second) baptism record.

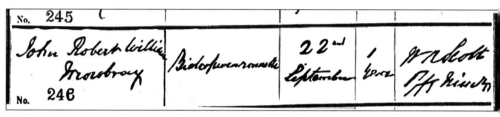

John Robert Mowbray baptism record.

By now William has left the sea-faring life and found work as a foreman at the local pit. The family moved to the Hendon area of Sunderland in 1863. Mary is expecting another child and, in November 1863, she is delivered of a boy, christened John Robert at Holy Trinity by the Rev Robert Waters.

Graves at Holy Trinity Church South Hetton, 2012.

This poor lad did not last long. He died of 'gastric fever' in September 1864. His death record wrongly names him John Robert William.

At the time of Mary Ann's trial, newspaper reports made many suspect something was amiss with the boy's death, especially when they linked it with the sudden death of Mary Ann's husband, William, at 39 years of age. However, there is good testimony from the doctor, Mr Gammage, who had overseen William's illness, that the death was natural, recorded as typhus fever.

> On the 22nd of September, 1864, a son, named John Robert William, about one year old, died, and on the 2nd of May, 1865, a daughter, named Mary Jane, died. The two last named were attended in their illness by Mr Gammage, surgeon, Sunderland, and he states that they both died of gastric fever. The deceased William Mowbray and his family were all insured in the British and Prudential Insurance Office, and on the death of her husband the prisoner got £35 and some smaller amounts on the death of the children …

This report in the *Pall Mall Gazette*, written at the time of Mary Ann's trial, clearly casts the aspersion that the deaths of the Mowbrays are linked to an insurance claim. The reporter gets some facts wrong and is joining in the hysteria that surrounded the trial. This hysteria sought to link every death around Mary Ann as an act of murder. This was without any sound basis in fact. Other newspapers joined in and reported that the formerly hard working and apparently fit William Mowbray was confined at home with a sore foot. Then on a Saturday night he suddenly developed severe diarrhoea, succumbed to a fever and by Sunday, 15 January was dead. This may be simple sensationalism, as William was certified as dying from typhus fever. He was buried at Holy Trinity, South Hetton, on 18 January 1865. The burial entry is incorrect as William was only 39 at death.

William Mowbray burial record showing wrong age.

The symptoms of this disease are very different from poisoning, particularly by arsenic. Typhus symptoms are abdominal pain, backache, diarrhoea, dull red rash that begins on the middle of the body and spreads, extremely high fever, hacking, dry cough, headache joint and muscle pain, nausea and vomiting. Arsenic poisoning involves drowsiness, headaches, confusion, terrible diarrhoea, convulsions, vomiting and blood in the urine. Whilst the symptoms of both illnesses have many things in common, what stands out is the rash in typhus fever and therefore it would be hard, though not impossible, for a doctor to mis-diagnose.

It is true that Mary Ann received £35 on William's death, plus small amounts for the children from Prudential Insurance. In today's money (2016) she would have received about £1,700. Mary Ann moved to Seaham Harbour and took a house at North Terrace in early 1865.

Four months later Margaret Jane, not having reached her fourth

North Terrace, Seaham Harbour, 2012. Mary Ann lived in the building beside the hotel.

No. 289

Margaret Jane Mowbray (second) burial record.

birthday, also succumbed to what was said to be typhus fever. She joined her father and siblings, being laid to rest at Holy Trinity, South Hetton.

It may be that all the Mowbray deaths were simply a reflection of the severe Victorian living conditions of the poor. It has to be borne in mind that the 1800s saw epidemics of influenza, typhus, typhoid, smallpox and cholera. Lice, mice and rats were very common and they were carriers of all sorts of diseases. Housing was very poor for those at the lower end of society, with terrible sanitary conditions. Both adult and infant deaths were very common, with families experiencing multiple deaths over short periods. So the Mowbray deaths would not seem out of place.

In the summer of 1865 Mary Ann handed the remaining child, Isabella, now aged about 7, over to her mother Margaret. She, with her husband, George, took on the care of the child. We can only speculate as to why. Was it a genuine attempt to go and search for work? Was it a weary woman who had buried the majority of her family and needed a break? Or was it a flight from responsibility? The only confirmed facts about this period of Mary Ann's life are that Mary Ann Robson married William Mowbray and bore him at least nine children. At his death two survived him, with one dying shortly after. Everything beyond that belongs to gossip and speculation.

Chapter 3

George Ward

Mary Ann seems anxious to move on. It was also later speculated that around this time Joseph Nattrass was on the scene and the black widow courted a future lover and victim. Whilst a meeting between Nattrass and Mary Ann was possible, we have no evidence whatsoever of any relationship. What we do know is that Mary Ann took up employment at The Old Sunderland Infirmary. She took over the post of fever nurse from one Isabella Smith, noted in the *Northern Echo* as being married to Samuel Smith a fireman. Isabella Smith in later testimony for the trial tells us what she knew:

> I was nurse at old Sunderland Infirmary for a great number of years, and I left about 1865 or 1866 to get married. Prisoner [Mary Ann] came into my place when I left. Her name was then Mowbray. She took my place and remained about eleven or twelve months. A man named George Ward was a patient in the Infirmary when she was there, and she attended to him; and afterwards married him.

Isabella would go on to confirm that Mary Ann had access to poisons, which were clearly labelled at the Infirmary. Isabella makes the point that she herself could not distinguish which bottles were which, being 'not much of a scholar. A scholar would know poison as the name was on the bottles.' We know Mary Ann could read, and the inference was left in the minds of the court.

Mary Ann married George Ward at St Peter's Church in Monkwearmouth, Sunderland, on 28 August 1865. George was born in 1833 in Sunderland. He is one of the men in Mary Ann's life about whom we know little. However, a great deal is known about his final days because of a report in the *Sunderland Times*. In that report we find that George Ward suffered an illness and a Dr Dixon was initially called in to care for him. However, as his condition did not seem to improve, Mary Ann asked a former contact at the Infirmary, Dr Maling, for a second opinion. George's condition included nosebleeds and all the doctor's efforts brought no improvement. George constantly complained of tiredness and feeling weak. Dr Dixon, completely puzzled as to why George was deteriorating, looked to a common solution that was favoured in the 1800s, and instructed Mary Ann to apply twelve leeches to George's body. Leeches draw an average of 3gms of blood every fifteen minutes. With twelve leeches and regular nosebleeds, a weakened George would be losing a lot of blood. It appears that the situation was complicated by the wounds left by the leeches, which continued to bleed overnight. Dr Dixon's assistant, Mr Coul, attended next day to clean and dress the wounds. Dr Maling was again called in and this caused Dr Dixon to take umbrage and leave Maling the care of George. This dispute was referred to at the time of the trial.

> … she [Mary Ann] – a widow with one daughter – nursed in the hospital a man of the name of George Ward. On his recovery, he married his nurse. In the same year she buried him. Cause of death said to be typhus fever; symptoms same as if death had resulted from arsenic poisoning. The case of Ward, and the controversy to which it gave rise, in which Dir. Maling and Dir. Dixon were mixed up, created some stir in Sunderland at the time. Ward died, however, and the parish buried him.
> *Northern Echo*

It was sensationally claimed that the symptoms were 'the same as if death had resulted from arsenical poisoning'. The report also gets the cause of death wrong, stating '*typhus*' when in fact it was noted on the death certificate as English cholera and typhoid. Dr Maling remained in charge of George's care, but eventually he too decided to leave. He reported that Ward was beginning to display signs of paralysation in his hands and feet. Mr Gammage would later state he had also been attending George. His comments were reported at the time of the trial.

.... he [George Ward] died on the 21st October, 1865, aged 33 years. Mr Gammage attended him, and, although he was an ailing man, he considered that he dropped off very suddenly.
Northern Echo

Arsenic, given in small doses, can produce a condition characterized by a loss of strength, confusion and paralysis. It does raise the question of Mary Ann being responsible. Did both doctors have suspicions and want to distance themselves from the case? It might be helpful to look at the background facts. Mary Ann had taken work at the Infirmary as a nurse. From our modern viewpoint we can misunderstand this role. Florence Nightingale began to see the problems with nursing in the 1860s and she began the process of training and education to make nurses what they are today. In Mary Ann's day a nurse was used more as a 'domestic' who would have to clean, cook, and carry out basic patient washing. They would also carry out very basic 'nursing' instructions from doctors, which amounted to cleaning wounds, dressing and administering preparations or procedures. It was not very well paid. Records for the time show salaries paid were about £16 per annum – in today's terms (2016) that would be about £1,300 per annum. Mary Ann's income was replaced by 'poor relief', which the couple received when Mary Ann did not work. This was four shillings a week, again in today's terms (2016) that would be about £1.50 a week. Because of George's poor health, this low income became the norm. Mary Ann had always had better ambitions for herself. She liked to have money and the fine dresses that it could buy. She also enjoyed the company of men and, the evidence suggests, an active sex life. However with such an ill husband, there was no sexual intimacy in the marriage. Such a situation would have been intolerable for Mary Ann. His death certificate stated his occupation as an engine driver in a steam tug, a very low status job, and his marriage certificate bears his mark, rather than a signature. All in all, he was not what Mary Ann had aspired to in a husband. It may also be noted that at the time of Mary Ann's trial, George does not get a mention from her nor does he appear in any of her letters. The circumstances were ripe for disposing of such a liability, if that was how Mary Ann wanted to resolve the situation – and she had good access to poisons at the Infirmary. All this is circumstantial and with no autopsy, the evidence was buried when George died on 20 October 1866. He was interred in Grangetown cemetery. This is yet another death that raises questions about Mary Ann's involvement.

Chapter 4

The Robinson Family

J ames Robinson was born in Gateshead in 1833. By the age of 18 he was an apprentice shipwright at Pallion, living with his mother, Ann, and his father, William, also a shipwright. We also know from census records that James looked after his widowed mother, after the death of his father. James married his first wife, Hannah Vawer in 1855 at Gateshead. She was 16 years of age. She appears in the census of 1861, where her age is given as twenty-two. In November 1866, Hannah Robinson died and was survived by her husband James and five children: William Greenwell, 9 years old; Elizabeth, 8; James, 5; Mary Jane, 2 and John, only 9 months old. Such a situation must have been devastating for James, not only losing his wife, but also having to care for such a young family. Although James had three sisters, they had their own families and could not offer the constant care and attention his family needed. James had a very good job as a shipwright so it was with some urgency that he advertised for a housekeeper. We do not know how many responses he received, but one reply came from Mary Ann, using the name Mowbray not Ward.

James saw something in Mary Ann that he was attracted to. We know that she had a reputation as a woman who liked cleanliness and took care of her appearance. She would also come across as caring because she had the experience of the Potter children to refer to, as well as her own childrearing. We can only speculate as to whether Mary Ann's seductive powers were also at work. James appointed her as housekeeper and she moved in on 20 December. At the time of the appointment James' son, John, was very ill. He had been under the care of the doctor for some time, and on 21 December, the day after Mary Ann moved in, baby John died. In a later police deposition, James Robinson could recall these facts quite clearly because of his son's death. It was noted at the time of the

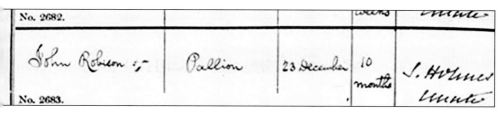

No. 2682.						
John Robison	Pallion	23 December	10 months	J. Holmes Curate		
No. 2683.						

John Robinson burial record.

trial that two surgeons attending both John and the children of Mary Ann were satisfied that their deaths were natural.

Only the most biased observer could attribute this death to Mary Ann, as the medical records are clear that his death was natural and he was already ill before Mary Ann arrived. John was buried by the curate Rev Holmes at Bishopwearmouth Cemetery on 23 December 1866.

Mary Ann settled into the Robinson household and, as may be expected of her, she made herself very attentive to James. So attentive that by March or April of 1867 she was sharing his bed. Becoming pregnant by James would very likely lead to marriage. Before then however, much more would unfold. It was in March 1867 that Mary Ann was informed that her mother, Margaret Stott, was ill at Seaham Harbour. We can only speculate at what Mary Ann thought of the news. She had got herself into a great situation, with a reasonably well-to-do man. She would not want anything to disrupt her plans for marriage. There was also the matter of little Isabella, the daughter she had left behind. Had Mary Ann told James about her? We know from the records that Margaret Stott was ill with hepatitis and no doubt in that day and age her death from the illness was pretty certain. The report in the newspaper was clear in pointing out the connection between the mother's death and Mary Ann's arrival:

A short time afterwards, the woman [Mary Ann] went to stay at her mother's at Seaham, assigning as a reason that the latter was bad. It is said her mother was able to sit up in bed when she got there, but that within nine days of her daughter's arrival she was dead.
Northern Echo

This clearly suggests the involvement of Mary Ann in the death of her mother. What we do not know is how long the mother had been ill. Was Mary sent for because the end was already near? It is true that, despite everything, Mary Ann did have affection for her mother. The dichotomy between wanting to consolidate her position with James and wanting to respond to her mother's illness would have been great. Mary did make the journey to Seaham, which is about 6 miles from Pallion. Her presence in the house may have caused tension with George Stott, because she had previously gone off and left Isabella with them. Mary Ann moved into her mother's house and, as a former 'nurse', may have been expected to care for her mother but by 15 March 1867, Margaret Stott was dead. At the time of her mother's death there was absolutely no suspicion that Mary Ann had murdered her. That allegation was made at the time of her trial and has stuck with Mary Ann ever since. However, if we examine the background to that time we may have to reserve judgment. Mary Ann was always close to her mother; Margaret Stott had once made the arduous journey from the north east to St Germans in Cornwall to get her daughter home and Mary Ann had responded in kind.

George Stott's story following Margaret's death can be traced via the census. In 1871, 1881 and 1891, he was married to Hannah, with a step-son, George Paley. The 1871 Census states the address as 9 California Row, Seaham.

George Stott with step-son George Paley and wife Hannah.

Their marriage took place in September 1867 and Hannah's name prior to that was Hannah Paley. The 1861 Census shows that Hannah Paley had lived with her husband in 9 California Row, Seaham.

Hannah Paley living next door to Stotts, 1861.

George's first wife, and Mary Ann's mother, Margaret Stott died on 15 March 1867 and was buried out of California Row in Seaham Colliery on 17 March. George Stott subsequently married his neighbour, Hannah Paley, just over six months after burying his wife. A quick courtship or did it start before the death of his sick wife? Then we have to remember Isabella. If Margaret Stott died, Mary Ann would be forced to take Isabella back to Pallion. What would be the implication for Mary Ann's future with James Robinson? Margaret Stott's death would not have been to Mary Ann's advancement. Furthermore, there was no financial benefit to Mary Ann. The real evidence, once more, is in a grave, this time at Christ Church, New Seaham. So did Mary Ann murder her mother? Perhaps, but as a Scottish court might decide the charge is 'Not Proven'.

It was reported that Mary helped herself to linen and other items from the Stotts' house, much to the dissatisfaction of George Stott. As we see below, the newspapers at Mary Ann's trial were highly emotive.

> In nine days she [Margaret Stott] was dead. Her death was sudden, the cause of it unknown. Mary Anne left the house, where her mother had died previously, stripping it of all she could lay her hands on. Laden with spoil, and bringing her daughter with her, she returned to Robinson's house.
> *Northern Echo*

These reports are heavily influenced by the hysteria at the time of Mary Ann's trial. Stating the cause of death as 'unknown' was not true; a doctor had certified the cause of death. Using the term 'stripping', gave the idea that she took everything, which was also not true. She had taken mainly linen. What we know as fact is that Mary Ann returned to Pallion carrying the goods from her mother's house and beside her was the young Isabella Jane Mowbray.

On her return to Pallion, Dr Shaw was called into the household. Young James Robinson junior had taken ill, followed quickly by his sister, Elizabeth. Dr Shaw would describe the children's condition quite graphically. The *Northern Echo* and *Morpeth Herald* used terms such as:

37

They rolled about on the bed
They foamed at the mouth
When given a drink of water, a hand basin had to be ready as they
'retched it up'

James junior was the first to go. On 20 April he became unconscious and died of what was described as 'continued fever'. He was 6 years of age. He was buried at Bishopwearmouth Cemetery on 21 April 1867 by the curate, William Ephraim Houldey.

His sister, Elizabeth, fought on but she too was overcome and died on 25 April 1867. Her death was attributed to gastric fever. She too was buried in Bishopwearmouth Cemetery on 26 April 1867 by the curate, James Holmes.

She was 8 years old. Neither James Robinson nor Mary Ann reported the death, we can only speculate as to why. The charitable view is that they were exhausted with grief and had asked Jane Hindmarch, the wife of a fellow shipwright, to do the duty, which suggests she was present at the death.

However, it did not end there. The child Mary Ann had brought back from Seaham also took ill. She was reported as having the same symptoms as the other children. Dr Shaw would also report that the child 'retched onto the face of the woman [Mary Ann]'.

The newspapers were very graphic.

Her [Mary Ann's] daughter struggled for some time, retching and working in fits, but at last she died. Cause of death, gastric fever, Dr. Shaw again attending. During the illness of this child it vomited in the face of its mother, who was immediately seized with the same symptoms, being inflicted with pains and fits.
Northern Echo

Apparently Mary Ann also took ill from this but she recovered quickly. Not so for little Isabella Mowbray. She died aged 9 years on 30 April 1867. Mary Ann was again reported to have been grief-stricken and the death was once again reported by Jane Hindmarch.

Isabella was buried at Bishopwearmouth Cemetery on 2 May 1867. The poor lass was separated in death from her other family, who had all been interred in South Hetton.

With such a steady stream of death, Mary Ann would later face accusations from all and sundry that murder was afoot and that she was guilty. Even her husband, James Robinson, made a statement at the time of Mary Ann's trial:

> I am convinced that my children were poisoned. I suspected it at the time, but I did not want my mind to dwell on the subject. They were healthy and strong, and only ill a few days before they died. Any time she gave them anything they vomited, and were sick and purged.

This seems strange and would appear to have been influenced by the events of the trial and newspaper reports. If he had been 'convinced' why would he continue to allow Mary Ann in his home with the other children and then go on to marry her? Also there had been doctors in attendance; did they too miss the evidence of poison if it existed?

His sisters also expressed similar opinions and when they read the reports of the West Auckland poisoning cases in the papers, they told him 'that was the way the children went'. One of them handed him a paper and said 'that is thy Mary Ann that has been doing that.' At the time they had not known that the Mary Ann in West Auckland was the same Mary Ann who had married their brother.

Hindsight confirmed prejudices that were already held. Did Mary Ann murder all these children? Again it has to be 'perhaps'. She would only have received a minimal amount in insurance money for her own daughter, Isabella, and the records show that James Robinson received the insurance benefits for his own children. James Robinson himself confirmed that Mary Ann was distraught at the times of the deaths. Was she simply acting? Why did she not kill the remaining two children, Elizabeth and Mary Jane? Mary Jane, at 3 years old, would have been an easy target; we must also remember the time in which the family live. Fevers and illnesses such as scarlatina, typhoid, typhus, and smallpox could attack a household and take away all children in the house. Mary Ann herself had contracted the illness. As with previous cases, the bodies were buried along with any evidence they might have provided. Certainly, in today's climate, multiple deaths would not be allowed to pass without an autopsy and inquest being held but it would be anachronistic to try to apply today's standards to that time. James Robinson, despite later statements of suspicion, went ahead and married Mary Ann on 11 August 1867, at the parish church in Bishopwearmouth. The marriage certificate shows that the marriage had issues surrounding it. Mary Ann was, at this time, Mary Ann Ward, yet she uses the name Mowbray.

James Robinson was probably unaware of the marriage to George Ward. Could it be that Mary Ann was concerned that James may be aware of the newspaper controversy in Sunderland about George Ward's illness and death? The two of them were living at the same address in Pallion, Sunderland, yet the addresses they gave were both false. He used Sans Street, Sunderland, and Mary Ann High Street West, Sunderland.

The only reason for this would be to pretend the relationship was morally and civilly correct, to avoid a scandal with the church authorities. On her wedding day, Mary Ann was over five months pregnant. The wedding dress would have been so arranged to avoid any bump showing. The vicar would no doubt have been aware and a blind-eye turned. It is also noteworthy that Mary Ann's signature is reasonably bold and strong, suggesting reading and writing were not a problem for her. This then raises the question as to why the letters from prison in 1872 and 1873 were badly written and at times used a mark rather than a signature. Was that a play for sympathy?

James Robinson has to be seen as an honourable man. He had lost his wife and watched Mary Ann go to Seaham and return, after burying her mother, with a child, which he seems to have accepted. He had lost two children and seen Mary Ann's child die. Despite all this he accepted his responsibilities for Mary Ann's pregnancy and went through with his commitment to marry her.

After the marriage Mary Ann settled into James Robinson's home. She was given control of the family finances, trusted by James to look after his financial affairs. She not only carried out the daily household finances, but paid into the building society, bank and Post Office savings.

Eventually, on 29 November, she gave birth to a girl. The birth certificate states the name as Margaret Isabella. However, the baptismal entry of 11 February 1868 shows the name as Mary Isabella. She died on 28 February 1868 from 'Convulsions – Not Certified'. The appellation 'Not Certified' was an indication that the doctor arrived too late to confirm the symptoms and cause of death. The death record has the name Margaret Isabella.

Meanwhile, in 1868, Mary Ann was pregnant again and, on 18 June, a boy arrived and was given the name George. The family now consisted of James and Mary Ann, William, Mary Jane and baby George. Incredibly, Mary Ann told James that neighbours were saying that she 'had not done to the children as she ought'. James reassured her that the rumours meant nothing and to ignore them. Again, a strange response of someone who was 'convinced' she had poisoned his children.

How Mary Ann treated James in response to his trust does not give her any credit. At the time of their marriage, James Robinson was in excellent employment with a good income. In good housing and with savings, the future for Mary Ann would have been quite rosy. It beggars belief that Mary Ann should want to ruin this setup. It was also around this time that Mary Ann was later accused of going to Newcastle to buy arsenic soap. We will look at this when we consider the trial.

James Robinson had to make a regular payment into a Mr Wayman's building society. It was reported to James that arrears had arisen in the account. In the other building society, run by a Mr Trewhitt, society officials were making up James's passbook when they discovered forged alterations amounting to £5 had been made in deposit entries. James Robinson entered into a dispute with the society, strenuously defending his wife's honour. When the society demanded the money be paid, Mary Ann lied to James and told him that the society wanted it paying the following week. However, James was alerted to an attempt by Mary Ann to secure a loan of £5 from a local loan company. She had tried to use the names of his uncle and his brother-in-law to secure the loan. James, by now reeling with shock and disappointment, was upset further still when he discovered that Mary Ann had also raided his Post Office savings account. Instead of £21 being in the account he found only 20 shillings. We can only imagine how James felt when his son, William, informed him that Mary Ann had been taking clothes, linen and furniture from the house for him to take to the local pawnbroker. Mary Ann had tried to tell

James that her father, meaning George Stott, would make it alright. James had made arrangements with Mary Ann to meet him at the savings bank, but Mary Ann did not turn up. He was finished with her. She had gone off and taken baby George with her. James Robinson closed down his house and moved into his sister's with William and Mary Jane.

It was New Year's Eve in 1869, when Mary Ann turned up in Johnson Street, Sunderland, at a friend's house. She had George with her. She told her friend that she needed to post a letter and went off leaving George in her care. She never came back. George was taken to James's sister's house and when James returned from a Watch Night Service in the early hours of 1 January 1870, he was overjoyed to discover his son's return, but also alarmed at reports suggesting George had not been properly cared for.

James now moved on to another home and in 1871 we find him settled at Bishopwearmouth.

1871 Census showing James Robinson now settled with his three surviving children.

James is not alone with the children. Amazingly, he seems not to have let the Mary Ann experience put him off housekeepers. He employed another housekeeper, Frances Pratt.

One puzzle is the question of what Mary Ann was doing with the

Second page of 1871 census showing James Robinson's new housekeeper Francis Pratt.

money. If she was spending it on dresses and clothing, James Robinson would have noticed this. There is no logical and obvious reason. Later reports, influenced by the trial, suggested she went to the races, but there is no real evidence of this in the record. One could speculate that Mary Ann was aware that the stealing was about to be exposed and was preparing for flight to another man. We can also note here that James Nattrass's wife had died shortly before this at Shildon. Could the rumours about Nattrass being her lover have started here? We will return later to James and his life after Mary Ann left him.

Chapter 5

The Lost Months

After leaving James Robinson, there is a period of confusion as to the exact movements of Mary Ann. Joseph Nattrass was a widower; it is possible that she could have turned to him, if she did in fact know him then. She gave her view of this period in a letter to James Robinson from her prison cell (written here with her original spelling):

March the 12

my dear frends

I so pose you Will mor than I can tell you con serning my Afull faite I have come I wish to know if you will Let me see the 3 childer as soune as you possible you can I should Like to see you Bring them if you can not Aske sum Won Eals to Bring them I have been told to day you say you onley had Won Letter from me since I left you if you have not got Enny mor they have been detaineg from you ie hope you Will get this And I thinke if you have Won sarke of kindness in you Will Try to get my Life spared you know your sealfe there has been A moast dredfull to hear tell of the Lyes that have been told A Bout me ie must tell you Art h Cause of All my trouble fore if you had not Left the house And So As I coud hav got in to my house When I came the dor i Was to Wandr the streets With my Baby in my Armes no home fore me no plase to Lay my head you Know if you call your mind Backe I shoud not solde my things in susicke street to come to you then I had mother to call on then But When you closed the dore I had no Won for you Know your sealfe I am Knot guilty of the Lyies

44

that has been tolde Consirning me if you spoake the nothing But the trouth I can not draw my mind on the past for it is mor than natur can bare Won thing I hope you Will try to get my Life spared for ie Am not guilty of the crime ie have to dyie fore consider things And do What you Can fore me so ie must Conclude A this time I hope to hear from you By return of post you K W… M A R M A Cotton

Mary Ann also wrote to Henry Holdforth, a miner and Wesleyan superintendent, who lived at West Hartlepool with his wife, Mary, and six children. We read of his report on Mary Ann earlier, and we know he knew the Robson family at Murton Colliery. He had obviously written to Mary Ann and her response was a longish letter, but the part about her time with James Robinson concerns us now (written here with her original spelling):

…the trial you speak of my dark eyes I Was happy then, and them Was days of Joy to all of our soles, but this Last 6 years my Life has been miserable sore I marriet a Man they call James Robinson, he had 3 sisters I never Was Looked on as I should be With nor of them. He said I could not Ergree We had sum Words a boute sum money and I Left the house for a few days, I did not Wish to part from him As I had no home I went to south hetton, stayed ther When I returned their was na home fore me he had sold What he did not Want And tooke the othe things and Went to Live With his sister so I mite go Where I Liked so I got mariet to this Man Cotton…

Remarkably, Mary Ann asserts that James was the cause of all her trouble and that she did not want to leave him. She claims to have wandered the streets in the letter to James but in the other letter she says she went to stay at South Hetton.

Chapter 6

The Cottons

I t may be useful at this point to place the Cottons in the picture. Frederick Cotton senior had been born in 1831, into poverty. He and his sister, Margaret, had been abandoned to the workhouse in Wisbech, without their parents. Margaret was born in 1832 and their lives started and ended in tragedy. She would become a good friend to Mary Ann as they entered into the world of domestic service.

Frederick Cotton senior had left the home in Cambridgeshire to search for work. As we saw in the census of 1861 there was a son, Frederick John, aged 13; a daughter, Margaret, aged 2, and another daughter, Adelaide Jane, aged 5 months. By September of 1863, his wife (also called Adelaide) had moved north to Sunderland and given birth to Frederick junior. Naming the child Frederick indicates that the other son from Cambridgeshire had already died. In 1865 another son was born and named Charles Edward. The girl, Margaret, from Cambridgeshire, also died on 9 October, aged 11. Then Frederick suffered another huge loss when his wife, Adelaide, died on 19 December 1869.

Charles Cotton, Frederick's brother, was a mariner and Mary would claim to have met him in Newcastle and had asked him to take the last Cotton child, who died in West Auckland. The tone of the letters and the absence of any mention of these things throw these claims into doubt. One of these letters was sent to the local newspaper.

112, North Woolwich Road, Victoria Docks, London, E,
9th October 1872

Dear Sir, - In consequence of the many reports which I have read, and which have (as it appears) been brought to light through your vigilance concerning Mary Ann Cotton, I am suspicious of her having had some acquaintance with my brother's family previous to the deaths of his first wife, two of his children, and also his sister, the latter having left her former service to keep house for my brother, F Cotton, about or soon after the time that the above deaths took place. At that time they resided at No. 5 Devon Row, Walbottle Colliery. I do not know any person who was living in the neighbourhood at this time, or I would write, with a view to obtain such information as might dispel or confirm my suspicions. My sister Margaret Cotton, as I was informed by my brother Frederick, died very suddenly with a severe pain in her stomach, but the other three had a more lingering death.

I am, dear sir, yours truly
Charles Cotton

A reply, written from Stanhope on 15 October 1872, to Charles Cotton, tells us that Frederick's sister immediately gave up working as a servant at this point and came to look after the dying Adelaide, Frederick and his family.

Stanhope Rectory, Darlington,
15th October 1872

Mr C Cotton

Sir, - I have seen your letter of the 9th instant in the *Newcastle Daily Journal* of to-day, and I write to say that your late brother Frederick wrote to me about his sister Margaret's death. She died, he said, after a very short illness. She left our service to keep house for her brother Frederick at Walbottle, as his wife was then in a dying state. I have reason to believe that Margaret had about £60 in the bank when she left us. She used to speak to her fellow servants here of this woman Mowbray. Margaret was an excellent servant to us as laundry maid, and we were sorry to lose her services, and still more sorry to hear of her unexpectedly being taken away. You can make what use you please of this letter.

Yours faithfully
Charles Clayton – Rector of Stanhope
P.S. Your sister came to us in July, 1866, and left us in December 1869

This was in response to the letter Charles Cotton had sent to the police (above) and was published in the newspapers. Charles Cotton also sent a second letter to the police.

Two things are of interest at this point, however; Mary Ann abandoned baby George in December at Sunderland and Margaret Cotton left Stanhope in the same month. Reverend Clayton confirms that Margaret knew Mary Ann and spoke of her in the household. It is not too far-fetched to say that Margaret and Mary Ann may have kept in touch. I believe we can ignore much of the sensationalism of the newspapers at the time of Mary Ann's trial about this period of her life. These claims involved prostitution and loose living, both of which are unlikely. Mary Ann had many faults but she was always capable of surviving by gaining employment. The separation from James Robinson may have happened in November 1869. We know from the records that in late 1869 she did work at a laundry in a hostel for distressed women in Sunderland, being employed by Edward Backhouse. Backhouse was a County magistrate and banker who lived in the very grand Ashburne House in Sunderland. He died in 1879 and spent around £10,000 per year on charitable causes. He was active in contacting the Home Secretary pleading for Mary Ann's life after her conviction. Margaret Cotton was a laundry maid at Stanhope. Did she get Mary Ann her laundry job?

It is likely that, with the combination of Margaret Cotton moving to Walbottle, near Newcastle to be with her brother, and Mary Ann on the lookout for another husband, that Margaret invited Mary Ann to come and visit her. She might even have looked to Mary Ann as someone who, as a former nurse, might help with the difficult situation in the Cotton household. This is even more plausible when we discover that, on 29 January 1870, Adelaide Jane, Frederick's last daughter, died of typhus.

Within three months, on 25 March, Margaret Cotton died from pleuropneumonia. She had savings of £60 at the time of her death, not an inconsequential amount in those days. It may be an uncomfortable thought, but is it likely that the loss of his sister was a devastating blow to an already shattered Fredrick and that the wily Mary Ann knew how to give comfort? Hadn't James Robinson also been the receiver of such comfort? We know that Mary Ann was delivered of a boy in February 1871, which would indicate conception around April or May 1870. Frederick Cotton accepted responsibility for the baby and therefore we can place Mary Ann in Walbottle around that time.

It may well be that April is the correct month and something happened to cause Mary Ann to move to Spennymoor where she began working for a Dr Hefferman. The census of 1871 tells us that Hefferman resided at number 7, Whitworth Terrace in Spennymoor. Mary went to this address to live and work in April 1870.

We do know that a letter was written by a Mr Gallon which read:

Fred's wife and daughter died in December 1869. The next daughter died in January 1870 and his sister Margaret died in February or March 1870. Mary Cotton did not come until the July following so she could have nothing to do with the death.

It is probable that Mary Ann was not resident at Walbottle, but simply an overnight visitor. The facts would suggest that Mary Ann did have knowledge of the household, certainly before the death of Margaret and possibly even before the death of Adelaide Jane. This was also what Charles Cotton, Frederick's brother, thought when he later wrote to Sergeant Hutchinson at West Auckland.

> 112 North Woolwich Road,
> Victoria Docks, London, E,

17th October 1872

Dear Sir,
I herewith send you a copy of a letter which I received yesterday, and which confirms my suspicions as regards the woman Mowbray (now known as Mary Ann Cotton) having had some acquaintance with my brother Frederick's family previous to the death of my sister Margaret,
Yours truly,
Charles Cotton

> Mr Hutchinson, Sergeant of Police.
> West Auckland

Of course, when Mary Ann came to public attention, the outcry was that she had done away with the Cottons in order to marry Frederick. However, we need to stand back and see that the deaths were probably due to natural causes. Certainly Margaret's death could not be confused with poisoning because the cause of death was specifically certified as pleuropneumonia.

We know that pigs were present near the Cotton's house and these animals were prone to catching a form of pleuropneumonia. The pathogens involved rarely transmit to humans though it can happen. Tales circulated later suggest that the pigs had been poisoned, but it is more likely they died of pleuropneumonia, which also killed Margaret.

We can, therefore, suggest that Mary Ann did visit the Cottons and begin a relationship with Frederick in early 1870. Her move to Spennymoor could have come before Mary Ann had realised she was pregnant. What we do know is that, while at Spennymoor, the light-fingered traits Mary Ann had shown with James Robinson had not gone away. Dr Hefferman would appear to have left much of the activity around the house to his assistant, Dr Brereton, and Mary Ann took full advantage. As Mary Ann became aware of her pregnancy, she would realise that, before too long, she would lose her post. Plans had to be made and it was then that the household began to lose various items, in a similar way to the Robinson household, when Mary Ann lived there. Reports say that the doctor confronted Mary Ann, who of course denied all knowledge of any missing goods. The police were not called in and two people were dismissed: Mary Ann and a groom, who also worked for the doctor. Does this suggest the groom and Mary Ann were in collusion and even in a relationship? We know Mary Ann's apparent need to have men fall in love with her. It may even be suggested that the groom could have been the father of the child that Frederick Cotton would take as his own. During her time with Dr Hefferman, and with the run of the place, Mary Ann had access to the surgery and clinic, where poisons would have been available.

The records show that in June 1870, Mary Ann left the Spennymoor house and turned up in Walbottle in July. It may be then that she reminded Frederick of their shared passion back in April. She was now carrying a baby – a result of that occasion? Or, as suggested above, Mary Ann could have had a relationship with the groom and was herself unsure as to the father. Either way, if Frederick was willing to accept responsibility, Mary Ann was content. At this point she was made 'housekeeper' to Frederick and settled into the domesticity of life at Walbottle. What Fred did not know was that Mary Ann was married to James Robinson and had not obtained a divorce. In this ignorance, he agreed to marry Mary Ann and on 17 September 1870, Frederick and Mary Ann were married at St Andrew's Church, Newcastle. She signed the register as Mary Ann Mowbray and gave her status as widow. There is no argument here that Mary Ann Robinson did in fact commit the crime of bigamy.

As a side note, the bigamy laws brought into force in the 1600s carried the penalty of hanging on conviction. By the 1800s this would have been a sentence of penal servitude for between two and seven years. Mary Ann was taking a huge risk in 'marrying' Frederick Cotton. Furthermore, as the 'marriage' was illegal, she would have no right to use the name 'Cotton'.

Walbottle was not a good place for Mary Ann. She was apparently disliked by neighbours. Stories of poisoning pigs etc. did not arise until after she was arrested in West Auckland, and were a re-interpretation of facts. As explained above, the deaths of the pigs were probably from an earlier time and from natural causes; only after Mary Ann began to get the reputation as poisoner did those with grudges find ammunition for their bad relationships with Mary Ann. On 8 February 1871, Mary Ann gave birth to a boy. She named him after her dead brother, Robert Robson Cotton.

The 1871 Census shows them at Walbottle on 2 April 1871, at Devon Row. People could count, and the birth, a mere five months after her marriage, would set many tongues wagging. No doubt Walbottle became a place of great stress for the family. In the mining industry, miners were bonded annually and this hated practice was not abolished until 1872. The bond was usually signed on 5 April each year. It is likely that Frederick could not leave Walbottle until the close of his bond on 5 April 1871.

Dr Kilburn, who testified at Mary Ann's trial, gave April 1871 as the date on which Mary Ann arrived in West Auckland and he became the family doctor.

Chapter 7

Deaths at West Auckland

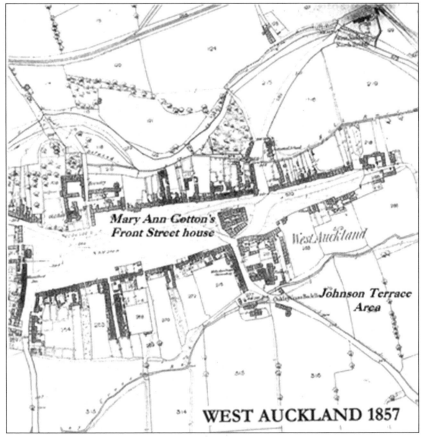

West Auckland in 1857 with Mary Ann's last home on Front Street.

When the Cottons arrived in West Auckland, they settled into 20 Johnson Terrace, a row of houses off what is now Chapel Street/Darlington Road. A good idea of the conditions there can be seen in this aerial photograph from 1964.

Johnson Terrace (on the right) in 1964. This is where Mary Ann first lived when she arrived in West Auckland.

Johnson Terrace now gone and replaced with allotments, 2012.

The area was regenerated in the 1970s and is now a field and allotments. We also know from the 1871 Census that Joseph Nattrass lived along the terrace from the Cottons, with the Shaw family, as a lodger. Nattrass was born in 1836 at Coxhoe. In 1860 Nattrass had fallen in love with a girl called Catherine Thubron from Pittington, a village about 6 miles from Coxhoe. They were married at Dalton Le Dale in October that year. The 1861 Census shows the newlyweds living with Catherine's family at the Pattison's Buildings in Seaham Harbour. Speculation at the time of the trial was that Mary Ann had an affair with him around 1861. There is no proof of such a meeting between them. Nattrass and his wife moved to Shildon, near West Auckland, where Nattrass took up an underground job at the local pit. His wife died in 1868 and after her death he moved to West Auckland and was now romantically linked, in village gossip, to Mary Ann.

Before turning to the various court appearances and all they brought out, it is worth considering the definite facts. Frederick Cotton was a hewer at the colliery and would have been a fit and healthy man to cope with the rigours of his work. In September 1871, he took ill at the pit and within a fortnight had died at the age of 39. The doctor attending had no

Frederick Cotton Senior's medical certificate days before he died.

54

Inside St Helen's Auckland church.

problem certifying the death as natural. The death certificate stated the cause as 'Typhoid fever and hepatitis 14 days certified' and dated the death as 20 September 1871. The medical certificate certifies the same.

Frederick was buried at the Paris Church Graveyard in St Helen's Auckland. Mary Ann was noted to be affected by the death and as things moved on, Mary Ann was very much accepted as a grieving widow. Just before Christmas of 1871, Joseph Nattrass moved into Mary Ann's house as her lodger. Ostensibly, Mary Ann was supplementing the meagre income she was earning through 'nursing' jobs. As Joseph Nattrass settled in, Mary Ann also took in the Taylor brothers, George and Edward, as lodgers.

In March 1872, young Frederick Cotton junior took ill and on 10 March he died of gastric fever. Another death for Mary Ann and the village folk continued to view her with pity. Frederick Cotton junior was also buried at St Helen's Auckland.

Before March was out, Mary Ann had lost another child. Robert Robson Cotton was certified as dying on 28 March from 'teething 3 weeks convulsions'. These tragedies, as they were seen by the village, had moved them with compassion. The coal company had allowed Mary Ann to live rent free and supplied free coal on the death of Frederick senior. The people of the village organised a subscription (collection) to which the coal company also contributed.

The Prudential Insurance Company had insured these three family members for small amounts – about £7. Around about this time, Mary Ann became pregnant again. We will consider this later when we discuss the child who was born in Durham jail. The lodger, Joseph Nattrass, was the next to take ill. He died on 1 April 1872 and the cause of death was certified as typhoid fever. He too was buried at St Helens Auckland. The Burial register shows Nattrass's entry immediately after the baby Robert Robson Cotton

Mary Ann benefited financially from the death of Joseph Nattrass. She received money from a Shildon Friendly Burial Society – about £15 – as well as clothing and a decent watch to the value of about £30.

By May, Mary Ann had packed up the Johnson Terrace house and moved with Charles Edward, to 13 Front Street, West Auckland. A Taylor brother moved with her. Nothing untoward was suspected and life moved on.

Mary Ann Cotton's house, Front Street, West Auckland (2012).

In July, the remaining child, Charles Edward Cotton, the last son of Frederick, took ill. On 12 July the young lad died. The boy was insured but the payment was never made to Mary Ann and we now turn to events that followed that death to discover why.

Chapter 8

Mary Ann Cotton's
Last Week of Freedom

I n summary; the facts which, when presented, do add up to pose a number of questions. Within a very short time frame, Mary Ann's husband Frederick dies; his son Frederick junior succumbs to an illness and dies. This is followed by the death of his step-brother, Robson, and within days of that, the death of Mary Ann's lover, Joseph Nattrass. We get a sense of the scene around these last two deaths from George Taylor, who was lodging at Mary Ann's house.

> …Nattrass was taken ill on Sunday. I did not know what the matter with him was. He went to work 2 or 3 shifts after being taken ill. Wednesday night I think was the last time he went to work. He said that he was very bad and would not be able to work again that week. I saw him again on Thursday; he was in bed then and seemed worse. He was upstairs then. I saw him once or twice again that week and he seemed getting worse a night or two before he died. My brother and I were called up by the prisoner who was in Nattrass's room. We got up and when we were going into the room prisoner who was by the bedside held up her hand to stop us going in. She was very red in the face and her hair was down her back. Nattrass was lying on the bed and his eyes were working. He died on Easter Monday. The child Robert Robson Cotton who died on Thursday before was lying dead in the same room as Nattrass…

This gives a great sense of the conditions that must have been around the house over the weeks of the different deaths. The stench of death hung over the place and Taylor's picture of a red-faced, bedraggled Mary Ann would reinforce the gossip of a raving serial killer.

These two deaths leave Mary Ann with one step-child, Charles Edward, who she wanted to commit to the workhouse. Within days of her request being refused, the boy was taken ill and died. All of these deaths are attended by doctors and all are accepted as of natural causes. However, there is one person in the village who finds the decision to certify the death of Charles Edward as 'natural' unacceptable – Thomas Riley. His protests to the police set in motion a train of events that eventually led to the arrest of Mary Ann Cotton.

Thomas Riley was a notable member of the West Auckland community. In 1851 he was the village's local butcher but by 1861 he had also become a farmer and employer of labour, with 100 acres of land in addition to his butcher's shop. In 1871, at the time Mary Ann arrived in West Auckland, he had 20 acres of land and his shop had expanded into a drapery, grocery and druggist. He was married to Margaret Riley, who was not present in the 1871 Census, but does appear in the 1881 Census. Some have confused this and assumed she was dead at the time Mary Cotton was in West Auckland. They had seven children. In 1871 he was also the overseer of the Parish Relief and the workhouse. He was the one who had suspicions that something might be amiss about the death of the young Charles Edward Cotton. He reported his concerns to Sergeant Hutchinson and to Dr William Byers Kilburn, the Cotton family's doctor.

Dr Kilburn had determined the boy's death was from natural causes but, because of Thomas Riley's intervention, Sergeant Hutchinson spoke with Dr Kilburn and the Coroner was informed of their concerns. Mary Ann was refused a death certificate on the Friday.

Sergeant Hutchinson called round to Mary Ann's house on the Saturday,

…on the 13th July I told the prisoner that it [the inquest] was going to take place, she asked me why. I told her because the doctor who had attended the boy had refused to grant a Certificate for his burial she said 'Oh people are saying I have poisoned him but I am clear I have made application to Mr Riley and the Relieving offices to get him into the workhouse but I have not got him in I have also written to an uncle of the boy up south for him to take him but he will not I am only a step-mother to him I have no right to keep him he has prevented me from earning many a pound I had a great deal of trouble with Cotton's family with so many of them dying in such a short time.

An inquest was ordered and Dr Kilburn carried out a hurried autopsy on the boy's body on the morning before the inquest.

We have to bear in mind that this post mortem was carried out on the table in Mary Ann's house. This room had the green wallpaper that was common at the time. This paper contained arsenic which could flake into the atmosphere. It was later argued that any arsenic contamination from the walls etc. could have compromised the samples taken.

The inquest convened under the deputy Coroner, Thomas Dean, and was held in the Rose and Crown public house next door to Mary Ann's house (the Rose and Crown has long since disappeared). Because the result of the post mortem was death by natural causes, the inquest had no choice but to accept Dr Kilburn's conclusions. After an hour, the verdict was returned that Charles Edward Cotton had died from natural causes. A death certificate to that effect was issued and the body of Charles Edward could be buried. Mary Ann immediately wrote to Thomas Riley. She made it clear that, as overseer of poverty relief, he would have to attend to the boy's funeral, as she was not able to arrange it.

Thomas Riley did not dispute about the burial and he made arrangements for the funeral on the Monday morning at the expense of the Parish. As Mary Ann watched the coffin of her step-son lowered into the grave, she may have thought her troubles were over. She was wrong.

Due to Thomas Riley being particularly vociferous in his continual refusal to accept the inquest's verdict of natural causes, the village was rife with rumours. Mary Ann was now in the spotlight of public scrutiny. After the funeral of the boy Charles Edward, Mary Ann prepared to leave the village. She called in a man, Lowrey, who had wanted to lodge with her and explained she wanted to move. She asked if he would take her furniture off her hands for £10. He advised her that leaving would only reinforce the village gossip, but if she wanted to sell then he would buy some of the furniture. He agreed to take items to the value of £3 19s 6d.

He paid her £2 9s 6d immediately and would pay the rest in instalments. (The balance was in fact paid as a lump sum after her arrest to help with her defence costs). On the Tuesday, Mary Ann looked to raise more money and called in her old friend and former neighbour Mrs Dodds. She took a 'handsome paisley shawl, some silk dresses and other articles' that cost £5 to the pawnshop. Mary Ann's moving fund was growing, but her time was running out.

Mary Ann was furious with Thomas Riley and made her bitterness known to those in West Auckland who would listen. It was also rumoured, without any evidence, that Riley was attracted to Mary Ann. It is most certain that Mary Ann Cotton would not have been charged, found guilty and executed, if he had not insisted the original natural cause verdict was wrong.

In essence, Mary Ann had given birth to over twelve children and was now forty which was considered old at that time. The only child she had responsibility for was Frederick Cotton's son and she had made it clear that he was not hers. Before he died, Joseph Nattrass had plans to marry Mary Ann and it was well known in the village that they had a relationship.

Brookfield Cottage, West Auckland (2012).

There had also been an excise man in the village named Quickmanning by most commentators on Mary Ann Cotton. He was reputed to have lodged in Brookfield House (called Brookfield Cottage in many reports) just along from Johnson Terrace. It was a very good house, certainly better than the terraces around it. It still stands today. What was certain is that a rumour had gone round that the excise man was interested in Mary Ann. An excise man certainly was a catch for Mary Ann and would have returned her to the same high status as that she had had with James Robinson. Although there is no evidence that the rumour was true, Mary Ann certainly played on it and, as Thomas Riley's deposition shows, she neither confirmed nor denied it. It seems likely that the boy, Edward Cotton, was in the way of Mary Ann's ambitions. Her request to get him into the workhouse was her first attempt to solve the problem, his death was very opportune and Mary Ann wanted to claim the insurance pay out. Thomas Riley's intervention upset those plans.

Dr Byers Kilburn had kept the contents of Edward Cotton's stomach from the post mortem and, on the Wednesday after the inquest, he subjected them to the Reinsch test for arsenic. This test requires very clean conditions to be observed. The matter to be examined would be mixed with a quantity of hydrochloric acid in a clean flask and be subjected to heat until boiling point was reached. A clean piece of copper foil would be put into the mixture and any arsenic present would adhere to the foil. Kilburn carried out this test at his home and there is no guarantee that contamination was prevented. He had so far shown a lack of ability in terms of procedure. However, he states, '...it gave indications of the presence of arsenic'. He then informed Superintendent Henderson of his findings.

On the following day, Thursday, 18 July, Henderson went to the Front Street house, where Charles Edward Cotton had died, and arrested Mary Ann for his murder.

The superintendent made a sworn deposition that describes what happened:

I am superintendent of police at Bishop Auckland. On the 18th July [Thursday] last I received a warrant for the apprehension of the prisoner charging her with the wilful murder of Charles

Edward Cotton. I went to her home on that day, read the warrant to her, to which she made no reply. I then with sergeants Harrison and Hutchinson in the presence of Dr Kilburn searched the home for poison. We found several articles which we submitted to Dr Kilburn, they were afterwards sealed and labelled and given to Sergeant Hutchinson.

The story continues in Sergeant Hutchinson's deposition referred to earlier,

On the 18th July last I was in the company with Superintendent Henderson and assisted in searching the prisoner's house and took from him some powders and pills which he handed me and which we found. I parcelled them up and sealed them.

Mary Ann was taken to the police station in Bondgate, Bishop Auckland, and the following day, Friday, 19 July, she appeared in the upstairs room of the police station and was there remanded into the custody of Durham jail to await a committal hearing.

That afternoon, William Dale Trotter, the clerk to the Justices of the Peace at Bishop Auckland, wrote to the Home Secretary, requesting an order for the exhumation of the body of young Charles Edward Cotton. The grounds given for this was the evidence of Dr William Byers Kilburn. Although the inquest jury had returned a verdict of natural causes, suspicion had arisen about the death of Charles Edward Cotton and others from the household. The village gossip, fuelled by sensationalist stories of Mary Ann's arrest in the local newspapers, had turned that suspicion into a certainty of guilt in the minds of the public. On 26 July, Sergeant Hutchinson, Thomas Riley, Dr Kilburn and Dr Chalmers and others gathered at St Helen's Auckland Churchyard to exhume the body of Charles Edward Cotton.

Because the sites of graves for parish burials were not marked, a number of bodies were exposed. The young lad's body was taken to a nearby empty house. The viscera and tissue that were removed were put into clean glass bottles by Dr Kilburn. He corked and sealed them and placed signed labels on them. These, along with the stomach that had been dug up from Kilburn's garden and the contents that remained after

The graveyard at St Helen Auckland where the Cottons and Joseph Nattrass were buried (2012).

Kilburn's analysis, were also bottled. A sample of the boy's faeces was also included. All these were given to Sergeant Hutchinson, who would take them to Dr Scattergood in Leeds. All of this would be confirmed in sworn statements.

William Byers Kilburn stated,

On the 26th of July last I was present at St Helens Churchyard and saw the coffin containing the body of deceased [Edward Charles Cotton] taken into an empty house adjoining. I opened the chest and abdomen and removed the viscera these I placed into clean empty bottles corked them with clean corks tied them down sealed them and under the seal of each bottle I placed a slip of paper with my own name, I labelled and numbered the bottles and gave them to Sergeant Hutchinson. A small parcel containing a napkin that I had received from Ann Dodds and which I had in my possession locked up I also gave to Sergeant Hutchinson, on the same morning the stomach and parts buried in the garden from my assistant Mr Chalmers I also put them into a clean glass bottle and sealed them in the same manner as the others and gave it also to Sergeant Hutchinson. The remaining portion of the contents of the stomach I placed in a clean glass bottle and I corked and sealed in the same manner as the others and gave to Sergeant Hutchinson.

In Sergeant Hutchinson's sworn deposition he confirms Dr Kilburn's statement and continues:

I took [the glass bottles and their contents] to Leeds the same day and handed them to Mr Lockwood a pupil of Mr Scattergood's at his residence.

Handing the items to Scattergood was the turning point for Mary Ann Cotton. He was the foremost expert in poisons. If anything was afoot, he would find it.

The investigation now turned to the questioning of other neighbours who were familiar with the Cotton household. At this stage, Mary Ann Dodds, Phoebe Robson, Jane Hedley, Thomas Riley, Mary McKiever, Sarah Smith, Mary Tate, Mary Priestley, Jonathon Watson Townsend the chemist, Mr Lockwood of Leeds, along with police and medical witnesses were being called to give sworn depositions.

Chapter 9

The Road to Durham Assizes

t was on 21 August 1872, in the elegant upper room of the Police Station Bondgate, Bishop Auckland, that Mary Ann Cotton made her appearance for the first hearing into the events leading to the death of her 7-year-old step-son, Charles Edward Cotton. She faced the two magistrates, Hick and Jobson. She appeared calm and held a white handkerchief to the side of her face throughout the hearing.

The first to give evidence was a friend and neighbour, Mary Ann Dodds, who had also cleaned the house for Mary Ann. She confirmed her sworn deposition by stating that she knew Mary Ann Cotton as a neighbour at Johnson Terrace and had been a cleaner for her when she moved to Front Street. She gave an account of Charles Edward Cotton's illness and death. She explained how she had washed the boy and laid him out. She also confirmed that she gave Dr Kilburn the napkin with the boy's motion in it.

....About dinner time Dr Kilburn's assistant came in and saw the boy and about two o'clock I went to Dr Kilburn's surgery for some medicine which I gave to the prisoner. The medicine was in a bottle and also a powder. On the following day I was at the prisoner's house and saw the boy. I asked him if he was any better, but he did not answer me. On the Wednesday I again went to the prisoner's house and saw the boy Charles Edward Cotton, he was then asleep. I thought he was worse and said to the prisoner, "I thought he would not be long here if he kept at that." The boy Charles Edward Cotton died on the Friday morning the 12th July and I washed and laid him out. The prisoner told me that the deceased had fits about twelve o'clock the previous night. The deceased died on a sofa in the upstairs room. He had previously slept in a bed with the prisoner…. At the time of the death no one lived in the house but the prisoner and the deceased, and the prisoner herself waited on the deceased.

She then made a statement that would become a focus of the case. The original deposition has this portion underlined by someone (possibly the prosecution).

About six weeks before the death of the boy I was at the prisoner's house cleaning I heard her request the deceased [Charles Edward Cotton] to go to Mr Townsend's shop for a pennyworth of soft soap and arsenic, the boy came back and said Mr Townsend would not let him have it. The prisoner [Mary Ann Cotton] then requested me to go for it and I went. Mr Townsend's son mixed it up and gave it to me. I took it back to the prisoner and she ordered me to rub the bedstead with it for destroying bugs. It was an iron bedstead – I rubbed the bedstead with the mixture that night and the next morning. I did not use all the soap and arsenic. I used about the better half of it and put what was left of it in an old pint jug and put the jug on a window sill in a lumber room upstairs".

Townsend Chemist on Front Street, West Auckland.

She went on to say that Mary Ann Cotton was afraid that they were going to take away her parish relief for the boy and it was very hard to keep him. She also confirmed Mary Ann wanted to get the child into the workhouse. She further stated that she asked Mary Ann,

> …if it were true that Mr Mann the excise officer would marry her if it were not for Charley as it was reported. She [Mary Ann Cotton] said Mr Mann liked the boy well and adored the ground he walked on.

She concluded by stating,

> I have never seen the prisoner ill-use the boy, but have heard her speak sharply to him.

The hearing then turned to Thomas Riley. He was on a personal crusade against Mary Ann and he wished to ensure that everyone knew of his views.

> I am Assistant Overseer and grocer and draper. On Saturday the 6th of July last I saw the prisoner [Mary Ann]. I asked her to attend to a small pox patient, she replied she could not because the deceased [Charles Edward Cotton] 'tied' her at home. She also told me she had applied to the deceased's uncle to take him, but he had declined, she also said it was very hard for her to keep the boy as he was not her boy and she had the opportunity of taking a respectable lodger, if it was not for him being with her. She also stated she had made an application for the boy to be put in the Workhouse and had been refused, and she wished me then to take steps to get him in the Workhouse. I told her he could not go to the Workhouse unless she went with him. I also said to the prisoner "I suppose you are going to get married to Mr Mann the excise officer. She said perhaps it might be so, but the boy is in the way, but he will go like the rest. I said 'nonsense' he appears to be a very healthy little fellow. On the Friday following I was passing the prisoner's house at 6 in the morning she was standing within her own door apparently in great trouble. I asked her what was the

matter. She said her boy was dead, and asked me to go in. I refused. I was considerable shocked at hearing the boy had died, and said "you don't mean to say the little fellow I saw on Saturday night is dead" I then went on. I afterwards went to the police and give information of the boy's death.

This was a powerful testimony as it painted the picture of Mary Ann being lumbered with a child, who was in the way and that she wanted rid of him. He conveyed his incredulity at the death being by natural causes in the hope that the magistrates would be of the same mind. Riley's testimony was the last that day. The case was adjourned as Kilburn was not available.

On the next day, Friday, Dr William Byers Kilburn was the first witness. To a packed court he confirmed his sworn deposition.

I last saw him [Charles Edward Cotton] on the evening of the 11th July last about six o'clock in the evening he was then suffering from vomiting some purging pain over the stomach not very incephant his bowels were relaxed his countenance was pale and waxy and the pulse at 120...

The doctor had sent him some medicine that morning, which was 'ammonia in a slate effervescence'. The six o'clock visit was because Mary Ann had sent him a message that the boy had vomited the medicine. He then gave Mary Ann another medicine, 'Bismuth and hydrocyallic acid' and 'some powders containing 1/8th of a grain of morphia' which was to be taken morning and night. This was the last time Dr Byers saw Edward Cotton alive. He continues to state that he carried out 'a post mortem examination'. His description of the examination gives a very detailed and graphic account of the state of the body and organs:

I made a post-mortem examination of the body of the deceased [Charles Edward Cotton]. The external appearances were emaciation, a good deal of distention across the bowels. I did not notice any contusions or marks at all of external violence. I opened the chest, the lungs were very adherent to the walls of the chest and there was some congestion of the left lung. The adhesions were indication of old standing inflammation. The heart was quite healthy. I then proceeded to open the abdomen and found the stomach distended with flatus.

He then comes to the stomach:

I proceeded to tie the ends of the stomach to secure the contents of it. The stomach was then removed and opened and the contents put into a jar.

He then continues:

I examined the stomach with a small microscope I had in my pocket and saw two or three particles of some white powder, which I thought might have been a portion of the last powder given him. My opinion at this time was that the child had died from natural causes, [The original statement is marked and underlined here] as I had not time before the Coroner's Inquest [which had been fixed to be held two hours afterwards] to make any analysis of the contents of the stomach and I formed that opinion chiefly on the ground that many Medical Authors state that the same appearance of the stomach are produced by the post mortem action of the Gastric juice upon the coats of the stomach.

He referred back to Friday morning when he visited the sick boy and asked for any of his stools that had been kept; he confirmed that Mary Ann Dodds gave him a napkin with a bowel motion in it. He said the napkin and faeces along with some viscera was sent to Leeds. He then states that he took the stomach, part of the liver and the contents of the stomach, 'a darkish looking fluid, about 5 or 6 ounces'. These he took and put in his house 'under lock'. When he heard the Coroner's jury ask for an analysis, he buried the stomach contents and other viscera in the garden and kept the stomach.

He then recounted the details of his test for arsenic on the Wednesday. Finally he confirmed that all the samples of tissue and fluid were sealed and given to Sergeant Hutchinson to be taken to Dr Scattergood in Leeds.

Kilburn was in an awkward position. He had a reputation to defend and his original conclusion of natural causes, especially following an inquest, now suggested incompetence. It became obvious that, as a result of his examination of Charles Edward's body alone, Mary Ann would not have been brought under suspicion. It was only Riley's insistence of foul play, and growing public gossip that brought about an investigation into Mary Ann's involvement.

Dr Chalmers, Kilburn's assistant from nearby Evenwood, gave his account of visiting the boy frequently during his illness. He was at pains to point out that *he* had not prescribed any medicines. He claimed that Charles Edward was suffering from gastric fever and that the medicines he was given should have relieved him, but 'they had no effect whatsoever'. His testimony confirmed that there had been five visits by the two doctors. They were convinced that everything was natural to the illness. Mary Ann had been active in getting them to attend and in asking for medicines to relieve the boy's illness. It does raise the question about her guilt and role in the boy's death. She certainly was not trying to prevent any external scrutiny of her care of the boy.

However, the next evidence would be that of Dr Scattergood.

He lived at 41 Park Square Leeds, with his two sons and two daughters along with his assistant, Lockwood, and three servants. His credentials were given as 'Surgeon Lecturer in Forensic Medicine and Toxicology at Leeds'. This was to underline the competence of his conclusions. He confirmed the chain of evidence of the samples from Kilburn; that they had been handed to him by his assistant Mr Lockwood, who had received them from Sergeant Hutchinson. He itemised the numbering and labels signed by Kilburn. All the bottles and containers 'were secure'. He stated:

> …I examined the stomach and parts of the bowels, the spleen, kidneys, heart and portions of the lung and liver purporting to be those of the late deceased. The parcel numbered 6 contained a napkin purporting to have in it the last execution from the bowels of the deceased. I have examined and analysed these….

He would go on to report his findings:

> ….inflammations of such a kind as are produced by an irritant poison.

Dr Thomas Scattergood.

He then specifically addresses the possibility of gastric fever as a cause of death:

> I carefully examined the small intestine to see if there were any appearances which are met with in cases of gastric fever but there

were no such appearances, the stomach and small intestines were well preserved so that the appearances of inflammation were quite distinct.

Then his evidence gave the hammer blow to Mary Ann:

I found arsenic in the contents of the stomach and in the contents of the bowel, in the substance of the stomach and liver, the lungs, the heart, the kidneys. I did not find any in the spleen. There were brown stains of faeces upon the napkin and in there I also found arsenic.

He was explicit about the quantities found, over half a grain of white arsenic or arsenic acid in the stomach contents and about a fifth of a grain in the other tissues. He confirmed that the articles taken by the police from Mary Ann's home contained no arsenic. He then made the very clear statement of his opinion:

I am of the opinion that death resulted from poisoning by arsenic.

This highly respected and eminent expert had concluded that Charles Edward Cotton had died from arsenic poisoning.

Mr Hicks the magistrate turned to Mary Ann and asked her if she had anything to say to the evidence so far presented. She had a very quiet demeanour at this point and gave a simple 'no' as her response.

There was no other course; Mary Ann Cotton was committed to be tried at Durham Assizes for the murder of Charles Edward Cotton by arsenic poisoning.

The charge sheet was drawn up and read as follows:

Mary Ann Cotton stands charged before the undersigned one of her Majesty's Justice of the Peace in and for the County of Durham this twenty-third Day of August in the year of Our Lord, one thousand eight hundred and seventy two for that the said Mary Ann Cotton on or about the eleventh day of July 1872 at the Township of West Auckland in the county aforesaid did feloniously administer or caused to be taken by one Charles

Edward Cotton a quantity of a certain deadly poison called arsenic with intent in so doing then and there feloniously wilfully and with of her malice a forethought to kill and murder the said Charles Edward Cotton and did then and there & thereby feloniously wilfully and of her malice aforethought did kill and murder the said Charles Edward Cotton.

This was then followed by the usual list of witnesses and warning before Mary Ann was asked whether she wanted to say anything. Her reply was recorded:

'I don't wish to say anything.'

She signed it by her own hand, Mary Ann Cotton.

This conclusion in itself could not convict Mary Ann Cotton. What they still had to prove was that she had deliberately administered it to the boy.

The interview of witnesses widened and sworn depositions were taken from others who knew Joseph Nattrass, or who had had contact with the other alleged victims. The Home Office lists of witnesses included: George Vickers, Thomas Hall, Elijah Atkinson, John Ayre, Robert McNaughton, George Hedley, some miners, as well as James Young from Prudential Insurance and Thomas Detchon, a chemist from Newcastle. The two Taylor brothers, who had lodged with Nattrass at Mary Ann's house, also gave their sworn depositions. Joseph Nattrass's doctor, Thomas Charlton Richardson, was asked to give an account of Nattrass's illness. Passages of his original deposition are also underlined, where he claimed to have had concerns about the death, despite saying nothing at the time.

As far the public were concerned, they had all the proof they needed of Mary Ann's guilt. They spilled out into Bondgate and the gossip flowed through the town as Mary Ann had to walk to Bishop Auckland railway station, subjected to the derision of the mob as she went. Mary Ann, her reputation already marred by accusations, had, in the minds of the public, been found guilty by the expert. She became the 'monster' whom parents would use to frighten their children into good behaviour.

Despite the weight of evidence that had already built up, William Dale

Trotter, Clerk of Justice at Bishop Auckland was not deterred from looking for more. The newspapers began to print articles questioning Mary Ann's history and there was a conviction in public opinion that others must have died at Mary Ann Cotton's hands. On 5 September, Trotter wrote to the Home Secretary demanding that, in the name of justice, further investigations be made into the death of others at Mary Ann's house. He sought, and obtained, permission to exhume the body of Joseph Nattrass.

It was on the morning of Saturday, 19 September that St Helen's Auckland Parish Church once more saw the exhumation of a body. The sexton of the church was unsure of the place of Nattrass's body and seven graves were opened before the body of Nattrass was found. Sergeant Hutchinson and Thomas Riley would confirm the body as that of Nattrass.

> I am Sergeant of Police, stationed at West Auckland and was engaged in the exhumation of the bodies at St Helen's Auckland on the 14th September 1872. On that day the body of Nattrass was exhumed. There was a coffin plate on the coffin. It had on 'Joseph Nattrass died April 1 1872 aged 35 years'. I have the coffin plate and have had it in my possession since. The body was identified immediately it was exhumed by Thomas Riley.

Dr Kilburn would give an almost identical description in his deposition. He added that, although decomposition had occurred, both the head and the body were 'easily recognisable by friends', suggesting others might have been present at the graveside. The features of Nattrass were also described by Kilburn as 'the head being lofty and a peculiar square shape, he was also bald-headed'. He would describe what happened to the body after exhumation.

> I then proceeded to open the body and internally the lungs were congested and hepatised and firm in consistence. There was a quantity of fluid in the cavity of the chest of a dark bloody nature. The heart was empty and healthy and its valves were all healthy. The stomach was secured intact and the lower part of it had a brownish red appearance externally, more particularly about the pylorus. The intestines were distended somewhat with gas and

contained a considerable amount of faecal matter and there were patches of redness upon the larger one. The redness externally had a brownish red appearance and contained a small quantity of fluid like faeces and was secured intact along its whole length for the purpose of analysis. The pancreas was healthy, the spleen very soft, the liver contained small particles of calcareous degeneration upon the surface and in its substance, otherwise it was of healthy appearance. The kidneys were healthy excepting the right one was much atrophied. The bladder was empty and internally healthy. Judging from the external appearance of the viscera I was of the opinion there was strong presumptive evidence of arsenical poisoning.

The good doctor was now able to see things with the Nattrass body he had been unable to see when he had examined the body of young Charles Edward Cotton. In the light of Scattergood's opinions about the boy, Kilburn was now free with his opinion; without carrying out any tests, arsenic was present.

Once again the samples were placed into clean bottles, as well as a sample of the earth taken from near the head of Nattrass's body. The stomach was placed between two plates and the parcels given to Sergeant Hutchinson, who took them to Leeds, this time personally handing them to Dr Scattergood.

Scattergood would again confirm the evidence trail and confirm that he had received the samples from Hutchinson on 16 September. He confirmed Kilburn's view of the health of the various organs except the stomach, stating that 'the rectum was likewise inflamed'. He also described the condition of the intestine and its contents adding crucially, 'none of the appearances characterised gastric fever were present'.

He ended his report with two important statements:

I examined the earth from the graveyard, it contained no arsenic whatever. From the appearance which I observed and from the result of the analysis I have no doubt the deceased died from poisoning by arsenic. I give that opinion with great confidence. I could not, judging from what I observed, say whether the poisoning was by one or more doses.

The magistrates at Bishop Auckland were now concerned that other deaths would need investigating. Their clerk, Trotter, wrote to the Home Secretary on 25 September, quoting from a letter that accompanied Scattergood's report.

> There is no doubt that Nattrass was poisoned by arsenic. I find there is considerable quantity in the stomach and bowels, between four and five grains of it being still in the state of undissolved powder – Arsenic in all the viscera.

He requested the exhumations of three bodies, those of Frederick Cotton senior and his two sons, Frederick junior and Robert Robson Cotton. He pointed out that information had been received about Mary Ann's past, which raised concerns. On 1 October, Superintendent Henderson sent his report to the Home Office. His report followed much of what we have already seen of Mary Ann's life before she arrived in West Auckland. The Superintendent took pains to highlight the parts of his report that indicated suspicions of poisoning. He also pointed out that Robinson, the only husband to survive, had forbidden Mary Ann from insuring his life. Trotter was keen to have other bodies exhumed in Sunderland. The Home Office would not oppose this, but did warn that the bodies would be in a very bad state because of the length of time they had been interred. Permission was given for the bodies in St Helen's graveyard to be exhumed.

The exhumations commenced at five o'clock in the morning on the direction of Joseph Drummond, the sexton at St Helen's Auckland Church on 15 October. There was quite a group present for the exhumation. The local Dr Kilburn was joined by another Dr Kilburn from Middlesbrough along with Dr Easby from Darlington, Dr Smith of Sedgefield Asylum, Dr Manson from Howden near Crook, Dr Thwaites of Bishop Auckland and a Dr Hinds. One wonders why so many medical professionals were present. It may well be that with so many deaths that were now suspected of being poisonings, they wanted to ensure no mistakes were made in the re-examinations of the bodies. Along with the medical men, The Rev S.J. Butcher oversaw the event as did Superintendent Henderson and Sergeant Hutchinson and, of course, Thomas Riley. The bodies of the Cotton children were found and identified quite quickly, young Frederick by the

Glengarry cap he had been buried in. Despite a ransacking of the burial ground over a long period however, the body of Frederick Cotton senior could not be found. By now the newspaper frenzy was increasing and Mary Ann's past was being examined. *The Gazette, Lloyds London Weekly, The Chelmsford Chronicle* as well as local papers all gave the story prominence. A typical example of the coverage appeared in the *Manchester Evening News* on 2 October:

THE WHOLESALE POSIONING AT WEST AUCKLAND

The woman Mary Ann Cotton, who is in Durham Goal on a charge of poisoning her stepson, at West Auckland, seems likely to be further inculpated. A Secretary of State's order has been received, ordering the exhumation of three more bodies, in addition to two previously disinterred. Besides the poison found in the body of the stepson of the accused, Mr Scattergood, of Leeds has also found arsenic in sufficient quantity to cause death in the body of a lodger of the woman, named Nattrass, whose death followed on that of one of her stepsons. The body of the boy was kept in the house a long time after death, and the woman, Nattrass died, adding "He (Nattrass) has gone upstairs now, and will never come down till they carry him out feet first." The man died complaining of terrible grinding pain in his stomach. The order of the Secretary of State, just received, is to exhume the body of Frederick Cotton, husband of the accused, who died 12 months since, Frederick Cotton his son, 10 years of age, who died in March last (another of her stepsons), and her own child, aged 14 months, who also died in March last. The woman has been married four times – under an assumed name on one occasion. The two first, and the last of her husbands are dead, but the third is said to be living. It has been shown that the woman obtained poison at different times. In the different places the woman has lived in the county of Durham the deaths are stated to have been numerous with those near about her, and small sums in most cases were obtained from benefit societies. She is between 30 and 40 years of age.

Anyone who had lived with Mary Ann and died while under her roof was considered a potential victim. James Robinson was interviewed by the *Sunderland Times* and his account confirmed, in the minds of many, the wickedness of Mary Ann Cotton. She was now being portrayed as a loose and predatory woman. In the midst of all this, concerns were being raised that Mary Ann could not receive a fair hearing. Even the Home Secretary in London was made aware of the concerns by a Durham man, H.I. Marshall, regarding the issues of bias in newspaper reporting. The Home Secretary, unwilling to restrict the press, dismissed the concerns.

As before, the bodies were taken to a house near the church and examined. The local Dr Kilburn put samples of tissues into bottles and various organs between plates. These had all been handed over to Sergeant Hutchinson who in turn handed them over to Dr Scattergood on 16 October. He carried out the usual examination and remarked on the parts that showed signs of inflammation. He noted that they 'were very characteristic of the action of arsenic'. He was once again made clear the original certified cause of death was wrong.

'I examined the small intestine most carefully for any appearances which are seen in cases of Gastric Fever and there were no such appearances whatsoever.'

He went on to describe his examination and analysis and his conclusion was clear, arsenic was found in all the viscera and in some of the body fluids. His conclusion was once again that the death of Frederick Cotton Junior was due to arsenic poisoning.

The examination of the samples from the body of the baby Robert Robson Cotton underwent a similar analysis. Scattergood found arsenic present in many of the samples. He was very clear in his conclusion:

I am of the opinion that the death of Robert Robson Cotton resulted from poisoning by arsenic. If he had died from convulsions from teething [The original certified cause of death] I should not have found the appearances I did. I have no doubt that the cause of death was what I have stated.

Scattergood's conclusions were definite. All the deaths he had been asked to investigate were caused by arsenic poisoning.

The continuing hue and cry was now frenetic in the newspapers. West Auckland became the focus for journalists from all parts of the United Kingdom. Even the papers in Guernsey were carrying the story.

By 11 November, all was ready to proceed with the charges of four murders against Mary Ann Cotton. Trotter sought a writ of *habeas corpus* from the Home Office to bring Mary Ann from Durham to face the witnesses from whom the police had taken statements. Trotter's ignorance of some aspects of law was exposed when it was made clear to him that the Home Office could not issue such a writ. He was directed to seek one from a local judge. However, Mary Ann was heavily pregnant at this time and delivery of the baby was expected within two months. She was under the care of the Durham prison doctor William Boyd. He issued a certificate to Trotter:

> I certify that Mary Ann Cotton, a prisoner in Durham Goal is in her seventh month of pregnancy, she is in such a state of health as would allow her to be removed to Bishop Auckland, but for her condition. It is uncertain how long such may continue.

Trotter now wrote to the Home Office asking for the trial to be postponed until the Durham Spring Assizes. There then followed a debate around who would bear the costs involved. Suggestions were made for committal hearings at Durham Goal but these were deemed impractical. The postponement was allowed. Money was not just an issue for the justice department; Mary Ann was also having difficulties with arrangements for her own defence.

It appeared that everyone was against Mary Ann. The newspapers were full of sensational headlines and people in the street made their opinions of her clear. Her committal for trial at Durham Assizes was, no doubt, a committal to the death penalty because it seemed there was no one on Mary Ann's side. However, that was not true. As would emerge later, there were people around who wanted to come to Mary Ann's aid.

Mary Ann's defence was a shambles. There were arguments over money John Leng of the Sun Inn had raised and how it was used. Then there was the ineffectiveness of her Bishop Auckland representative, Smith. Smith took it on himself to go to Mary Ann's neighbour, Mrs Dodds, and demand she give him pawn tickets she held for a shawl,

MARY ANN COTTON'S DEFENCE FUND.

The Prisoner MARY ANN COTTON, who is committed for trial for Wilful Murder in four cases to the Assizes at Durham, which commence on Monday next, is without the necessary means for her defence.

A large number of influential persons have expressed a desire that funds should be raised to enable her to procure a fair trial, which is the boast of our English constitution.

A committee has been formed for the purpose of retaining solicitors and counsel. Any one deeming it desirable will have the opportunity of contributing to the defence fund.

Mr. JOHN LENG, Sun Inn, 2, High Bondgate, Bishop Auckland, has kindly consented to receive donations on behalf of the committee.

As very little time is allowed for preparing the defence, parties subscribing will be kind enough to forward their subscriptions immediately.   2728

Appeal for funds for Mary Ann's defence.

dresses and other items belonging to Mary Ann. He also took back from Manning, the customs officer, the silver watch he held for Mary Ann. This was the one left to her by Nattrass in his will. According to Mr Lowrey, a former lodger of Mary Ann's, Smith had taken furniture and other items and had sold them in Bishop Auckland for £13. Lowrey had also bought items and had given Mary Ann a part payment, the rest he gave to Smith for her defence of around £7. After the first hearing Smith said there was nothing left. Mary Ann would later write from prison (produced below with her original spelling):

> I ingaeged A man they Call him Smith I thate he Was a solisete At frist Whun he come to me he got A bout £20 bloing to me for my first case he tolde me on the day I Was tryied At Auckland ie Was not t Speake A Single Worde And that mr Blackwell and Greenhow Would be thare to defende mee When ie Went in to the docks thore Was nowon for me the Jugdge A pointed the Counsler ie must say he was A clever man to for if he had My propr defence I should Won th tryile".

81

On 11 March 1873, she wrote about Smith to an old neighbour, who must have written to her after her trial. It was possibly Mary Ann Dodds, her neighbour and cleaner, who had spent a great deal of time with her. (Produced below with her original spelling):

But smith has Lead me rong he told me not to speake A single worde if I Was Asked Ever so if I hard Ever so mutch ie Was not to say it Was Wrong that would be All don in durham he has never Brote forth Won Wittness fore me he know What they Ware Wanted fore not only the childe but for my sealfe I do not Want nothing but the trouth.

This was raised at Mary Ann's hearing in Bishop Auckland. Mr Trotter, the magistrate's clerk made mention of this when addressing the Bench:

The prisoner, Sir, wishes to make application to the court. She states that a person of the name of Smith, by her authority, has sold all her furniture, for the purpose of her defence. He is not here – not to be got hold of – and she is not in possession of any money.

All in all a mess – Mary Ann's original defence team were a disgrace. A solicitor, Chapman, was initially to look after Mary Ann's defence. He never took any part in the hearings or Durham trial. Instead he appointed his clerk, Smith, who, as we have seen, took her money and gave her terrible advice. He had advised her that she was to say nothing and do nothing. Smith did not even turn up to the hearing. Chapman's behaviour in appointing a junior clerk and not being seen in public with Mary Ann suggests that he was too inexperienced for the case and did not want to be associated with such notoriety. He informed Mary Ann that he wanted to withdraw and that she should seek other representation. It was because of this that a Mr Charles Murray from Stockton, had contacted George Hedley, Mary Ann's neighbour, asking to be put in touch with Mary Ann's friends and promised that she would have able counsel at Durham. He wrote,

If you will be good enough to place Mrs. Cotton's friends in communication with me at once (say per return of post if possible), I will take means to have this woman well defended by able counsel [emphasised here by Murray] at the coming Durham Assizes.

His letter is in the police files and was reported in the *Northern Echo* newspaper in its report on the hearings at Bishop Auckland. Smith had been responsible for the pathetic representation in the first hearing. There is no record that he ever got in touch with Charles Murray, who we never hear of again.

The press would print a note from Durham Goal that showed Mary Ann authorising the sale of her furniture by Smith and his obtaining the furniture and key to her house, from Sergeant Hutchinson. Mary Ann does not give him any other authorisation to get the pawn tickets from Mrs Dodds or the watch from Manning.

Durham Goal, 28th July 1872

I hereby authorise Mr. George Frederick Smith to take possessions and dispose of my furniture, Mary Ann Cotton.

Received from Sergeant Thomas Hutchinson, possession of Margaret (sic) Cotton's furniture; also the key of the house. 30th July, 1872 – Geo F. Smith.

Mary Ann remained in Durham prison. Her Christmas in 1872 must have been a miserable one, heavily pregnant and well aware that her outlook was bleak. She felt let down by her defence team and the people she had expected to visit her had ignored her. During the harsh winter at the beginning of 1873, Mary Ann Cotton gave birth to a baby girl in the soulless confines of the Durham Goal. The baby's birth certificate confirms she was born on 7 January 1873, in County Prisons, Durham. She named the baby Margaret Edith Quickmanning Cotton. The birth certificate is interesting because Mary Ann does not sign the document, but puts an 'X', even though we know she could write a signature. No father is named and the column for mother's name states the mother as: 'Mary Ann Cotton, late Mowbray, formerly Robson'. Her married name of Ward is missing, as is Robinson. Mary Ann would have provided the information herself and we can only wonder why these two were left out. The newspapers were obviously excited by this development, of this 'monster' giving birth to a child. One of the local papers, *The Morpeth Herald* covered the event.

> It will be remembered that the woman Mary Ann Cotton, who was committed for trial by the Bishop Auckland magistrates about three months ago on a charge of poisoning her little boy, Charles Edward Cotton, was not arraigned before Mr Justice Denman at the winter gaol delivery for the county of Durham in December last, she being then bedfast; and it was then stated that three or four charges of poisoning against her had been delayed on account of her approaching confinement. The latter having occurred on Friday last, when the miserable woman was delivered of a female child.

Despite being in prison, Mary Ann nurtured her daughter throughout the time she was on trial and, while there was hope, she would not let her go. The arrival of the baby cleared the way for charges to proceed. The Bishop Auckland court contacted the Home Secretary on 7 February 1873 to inform him that there was enough evidence to have four cases of murder by poisoning brought and that Mary Ann could be considered a wholesale poisoner. Three days later the Home Secretary agreed and stated that, because of the serious nature of the case, the Solicitor to The Treasury should take charge of the proceedings, a decision that was taken as an insult by the local judiciary. On 6 March, *The Manchester Daily News* ran the story:

SIR JOHN COLERIDGE AND THE WEST AUCKLAND POISONINGS

> The *Daily News* has the following remarks:- Sir John Coleridge had directed the leading brief in the West Auckland poisoning case to be delivered to an eminent Queen's Counsel, of whom the worst can be said is, that he is not the Attorney-General of the County Palatine of Durham. The Bar of the Northern Circuit believe that the gentleman who holds the office has been slighted,

and they have taken the matter so much to heart that, as 'Junior' rather weakly intimates, contrary to their invariable practice, they held a Special Court on Sunday to discuss the question. The result of this discussion was curt and not very well-conceived letter of the 'Junior' to the Attorney General, in which the latter was requested to reconsider his determination, on pain of being held guilty of insulting the Attorney General of Durham and the Northern Circuit Bar. Sir John's reply is written in much good temper; but he hardly shows his usual skill, when he rests his defence on the absence of any right in the Attorney General of Durham to lead the prosecution in question. The wrong complained of is simply a breach of professional etiquette which the Bar represents with the vigour of a Sheffield trades union. It is satisfactory to find that Sir John promises to observe the etiquette in future, should he ever have the opportunity of directing a similar prosecution – a contingency which, with the cheerful optimism of his character, he regards as highly improbable.

The lawyers were fighting like dogs over the bone of what they knew would be a high profile case and one that, from the evidence, they felt sure they would win. As for Mary Ann, she was left high and dry by her defence team. The sworn depositions taken by the police were now to be tested in open court and, in those upcoming hearings at Bishop Auckland, there would be no one to properly defend her.

Around 6 o'clock on a Friday morning in Durham Goal, Mary Ann was made ready for the journey to Bishop Auckland. She and her baby were to be accompanied by Thompson Smith, head warder of Durham Gaol and Matron Margaret Robinson who was, by all accounts, a kindly woman. Mary Ann wore a smart black cotton dress and a black bonnet trimmed with crepe. She also wore a black and white chequered shawl, in which the baby would be enclosed for the journey.

The party travelled by train from Durham station. Word had got out about the journey and people gathered at the station to get a look at the notorious woman. Many more onlookers gathered at stations along the route, also wanting sight of 'The West Auckland Poisoner', as she had been dubbed. At Bishop Auckland the warder waited until the passengers had all cleared the platform – a simple act of decency to protect Mary Ann from immediate abuse. The party were provided with a bus that would take them to the courthouse. A large crowd had gathered along the street from the station to the courthouse, to gawk and to jeer.

Trotter was to prosecute the hearing and made a spectacle of the event – he was determined to have his moment of fame. He arranged for a row of chairs to be placed in the courtroom and designated them 'first class'. He gave tickets to the worthies who wanted to see the infamous woman. The 'second class' area was standing only and the lesser mortals would occupy this. He also allocated space for sixteen journalists.

One of those journalists was from the local *Northern Echo* and on 22 February 1873, he gave a good account of Mary Ann as she sat in the courtroom.

The interest of the public, however, was centred in the person of Mrs Cotton, who occupied a chair immediately facing the magistrates. On one side of the prisoner sat the prison matron; on the other the editor of a weekly contemporary. Mrs Cotton and the Matron alternatively nursed the child, which was on the whole, very well behaved. Considerable curiosity was naturally felt as to the personal appearance of the accused. Some atrocious representations of her face have been circulated, which certainly did her but scant justice. Mrs Cotton is not a woman of great personal attractions; but her features are not by any means as bad as we were led to suppose. Her black hair, brushed backwards from a rather low and slightly retreating forehead, was confined in a net. Her dark brown eyes were usually fixed intently on the witnesses in the box, occasionally gleaming curiously as anyone passed between her and the bench. Thin compressed lips gave a rather determined cast to her features, the only disagreeable expression of which was one of cunning. Her complexion was pale and clear. Although she has been married four times she only wore one wedding ring. Those who care about costume will be interested to hear that she wore a black cotton dress, a black and white large check shawl, and a black bonnet trimmed with crape. She was calm and collected, fully alive to her serious position, but in no wise disconcerted. Her baby – the luckless little mortal that came into this world on the 10th of January [the date is wrong] – is dark, with black hair. It wore the usual satin cap, trimmed with pink. It was wrapped in a shawl like its mother's. Mrs Cotton nursed her child part of the time. Occasionally she handed it to the Matron. It was very quiet, and was quite satisfied with the breast. The Matron, who sat beside the prisoner, from time to time explained the technicalities, which evidently puzzled her charge, who, we regret to say, was undefended.

This paints a good picture of Mary Ann, sitting undefended as an object of curiosity. With no legal representation, she relies on a nurse to guide her understanding of the proceedings. One wonders if this can be called justice.

The court eventually came to order at 11 o'clock and the first charge against Mary Ann was called. This was that she had, on 1 April 1872, wilfully murdered Joseph Nattrass, aged 35.

Trotter then took the floor. He reported to the magistrates that he was acting on behalf of the Treasury, who had already taken proceedings against the prisoner, which would be the subject of a case at the next assizes in Durham. He did not first address the case of Nattrass directly, but laid out the general reason for the hearing, which was to examine whether there was a prima facie case to bring her to trial, or rather to issue a warrant to detain her, for other murders. He stated that he would not go into detail on the evidence but would outline the cases generally.

Trotter then stated that Mary Ann had had four husbands. In one case, he pointed out, she had married whilst her previous husband was alive. Three of them had died whilst she was with them. The story of Frederick Cotton and his three children was then brought to the magistrate's attention. They were named and Trotter entered into the record that Mary Ann had already been committed for the murder of Charles Edward, with the two other children being subject to the present inquiry. He painted a picture of a woman closely associated with several deaths, one of which she was under suspicion of murder for. He then described Mary Ann taking in lodgers, one of whom had been Joseph Nattrass and it was to this death he now turned.

He described Nattrass as a pitman who had taken ill about a fortnight before his death. Nattrass, he said, complained of being sick to several workmates, but could not vomit. A few days before he died he took to his bed and was attended by a Dr Richardson for enteric fever. Trotter said he would call witnesses who would testify to Nattrass's sickness and suffering. There would also be evidence of a medical nature that would show evidence of slow arsenical poisoning. Trotter informed the court that the bodies of Nattrass and the two Cotton children had been exhumed by order of the Secretary of State and the contents of their viscera had been sent to Dr Scattergood of Leeds, who found all three had, 'without doubt', died from arsenical poisoning. Trotter knew that this fact in itself was not enough to bring Mary Ann to trial for their murder and he makes it clear that the evidence on its own was 'of a circumstantial character'. The question was, who had administered the arsenic? Trotter said that it would be shown that the only possible person was the prisoner, as she had been the only person to attend Nattrass. He claimed that when neighbours wanted to bring nourishing food to him, Mary Ann put them off. Trotter claimed he would further show that the prisoner was in possession of arsenic a very few days after the death of Nattrass. He then referred to witnesses who would testify that Mary Ann said she would not bury Robert Robson Cotton, who had already died on 28 March and was due to be buried on Saturday, 30 March, until Nattrass had died. She had even, he commented, sent for stockings to bury him even before he had died. These and other circumstances would seem to show she 'knew something more than any other ordinary mortals' that Nattrass was going to die. Trotter then began to call the witnesses.

First to give evidence was George Vickers, a workmate or 'marrow' of Joseph Nattrass. He stated his relationship with Nattrass, confirming he worked with him at the West Auckland Colliery. He went on:

> About three days before Nattrass give over working he complained of being very ill. He complained of being very sick but I cannot say whether he vomited. He also complained of being rather purged, he also complained of a twist in his bowels and he retched. The last day he was at work I walked out of the pit with him. He then complained of sickness, purging and pain in his stomach. He was very bad the last shift we worked together.

Thomas Hall, who was the overman at the colliery, confirmed Nattrass had worked under him. He confirmed he had been with Nattrass, the Sunday before he died, at the prisoner's house. When he was there he saw the prisoner attending to him. Thomas Musgrave, another workmate, was there with him.

Mary Ann was in the room. I spoke to Nattrass. He said he was really very bad. He did not complain of any particular symptoms. When I went on the Sunday to see him again I noticed that there was a dead child in a coffin in the same room with Nattrass. I asked Mrs Cotton and another woman named Smith why they did not bury the child. Mrs Cotton replied she did not intend to bury the child as Nattrass would not live long. I inferred from that that she intended to bury them together. He was off several shifts before he died. I think he would be off more than a week. I knew Nattrass fifteen or sixteen years. He was a pretty healthy man.

Phoebe Robson, the wife of William Robson, a neighbour of Mary Ann's was called next. She stated she had known the prisoner for some time and was in the habit of going to her house. She also knew Nattrass and confirmed he had been a lodger with Mary Ann for four or five months, moving in after her husband Frederick's death. She gave a similar account of Nattrass's illness and symptoms as Vickers and Hall had done. An important part the of testimony, for Trotter, followed.

Nattrass died on Easter Monday the 1st April. The prisoner's son Robert Robson Cotton died on the Thursday previously. The child was buried on Easter Sunday and Nattrass died on Easter Monday. Mrs Cotton attended Nattrass particularly closely. She never left his bedside during his illness. She was always about him and over him and would not let anyone else attend him. I many times said to the prisoner that Nattrass would be better if he had support. She said he could not take anything. I never saw her give him anything. During his illness he had fits. This was the latter part of his illness.

She then went on to describe him being severely held during his fit, and graphically described him as having 'scringed' hands [that is, his hands were curled into tight fists], grinding his teeth, turning up 'the whites of his eyes', drawing up his legs, and going stiff. These matters were mentioned to Dr Richardson. The doctor, she reported, had said 'I don't understand those fits'. Then she added more details that again would support Trotter's case.

> I was present when my sister-in-law, Sarah Smith, asked the prisoner if she would have the child [Robert Robson] buried on the Saturday. The prisoner replied she would wait until the Sunday. On the Sunday the prisoner said she thought she would let it be as Nattrass was not going to live long and she would have them both buried together.

Examined by the Bench she added:

> The first time I saw the fits was on the Thursday previous to Nattrass's death.
> I know nothing of any mixture from Jane Hedley.

Sarah Smith, the wife of William Smith, a miner, and sister-in-law of Phoebe Robson, then gave testimony. She again spoke similarly of Nattrass's illness, giving the same details and also the same graphic account of the fits as her sister-in-law. She said she went to visit Nattrass every day of his illness. She then continued:

> The prisoner waited on Nattrass very closely and did not leave him a great deal. She allowed no one else to wait on him. I asked the prisoner if Nattrass could take a little beef tea and she said 'no'. I saw Nattrass twice take a cup of tea and often saw him get drinks. The prisoner always gave him the drinks. Nattrass complained much of thirst. She had two small teapots on a table in the room and what she gave him was out of these teapots or out of a glass.

She went on to describe the visit of Dr Richardson, who when told about the fits, asked:

What kind of fits are they? He is always taking fits when I am not here.

She then referred to the stockings mentioned by Trotter:

On the Saturday previous to Nattrass's death I was in the prisoner's house when Charles Edward Cotton came in with a pair of stockings. The prisoner said to me if anything happened to Nattrass I have not a pair that would do for him.

Jane Hedley, another miner's wife and a woman who regularly visited Mary Ann's house was next. She again told a similar story about Nattrass's illness, adding that she had assisted during that time. She spoke of Mary Ann's role:

During his illness the prisoner waited on him and was constantly about him. I saw no one else wait on him. The prisoner gave him anything he required.

She went on to describe the fits in similar detail to the previous witnesses. She also described the conversation of Nattrass with Dr Richardson, when they disagreed about Nattrass's condition. Nattrass had tried to tell the doctor that what he had was no 'fever', but Dr Richardson replied that he knew better and that there was no use his coming to visit. Hedley said she had been present during the last fit Nattrass had during which he died. Then she gave details of a conversation she had with Mary Ann:

On the Thursday before Nattrass died the prisoner told me that Nattrass had said she, the prisoner, was to have his watch and Club money as she had been his best friend. On the same day the prisoner asked me to get a letter written for the burial money from the Club of deceased. I lived about a half a dozen doors from prisoner at the time. Shortly after Nattrass's death, namely about a week, the prisoner was in my house assisting to clean. She sent me to her house for a pot that stood on the pantry shelf. She said there was soft soap and arsenic in the pot. I went for and got the pot and showed it to the prisoner. She said it was the right one and what she got to clean beds with. The prisoner took out some of the contents of the pot and put it on the wall. There would be about two tablespoon full in the pot when I brought it to my house and the prisoner used about a knife point full. I kept the pot in my house for some time and then gave it to Phoebe Robson.

Trotter was using this testimony to show that before Nattrass's death, Mary Ann had access to arsenic and that there was a motive for Mary Ann to murder Nattrass.

Elijah Atkinson was now asked for his statement. He confirmed his trade as a shoemaker living in West Auckland. The 1871 Census however, gives his trade as a 'Pointsman'. He lived near Mary Ann's old house in Johnson Terrace, with his wife, Elizabeth. He signed his statement unlike the others who had only made their mark. He had been sent for on 28 March 1872, probably because he could write and was an 'independent' witness. George Hedley, Jane Hedley's husband, was with him. He told the court that he had specifically asked Nattrass if he wanted to leave everything to the prisoner. Nattrass said it 'was his desire, he had no friends that had ever looked at him'. Atkinson wrote down a will, to which Nattrass put his mark; Atkinson and George Hedley witnessed it and gave it to Mary Ann. His inclusion in the list of witnesses was, no doubt, to show motive for murder. He listed the contents of the will in his statement.

Nattrass had a watch which was hanging at his bedhead, £10 in the Odd Fellows Club [Lodge] held at the Dun Cow, Shildon. The money from the Club was payable at death, which I knew. The prisoner was present all the time I was making the will.

John Ayre, a coalminer, followed Atkinson. He was the steward of the Odd Fellows Lodge at Shildon. He paid out any sick or burial monies due to members. He said that when he received notice of Nattrass's death, he reckoned that Nattrass was due £10 burial money and 15s sick money. Because the prisoner claimed to be entitled to the money he paid her £5 15s. His fellow officer at the Lodge, Robert McNaughton, also a miner, gave witness to handing £5 to George Hedley to pay to the prisoner. Both stated that there were no receipts given, which was the practice of the Lodge. George Hedley confirmed that he had received the money and that it was handed over to the prisoner. He was re-examined and confirmed that the prisoner had asked him to go to the Odd Fellows Lodge to get Nattrass's money and that he had obtained a death certificate from Dr Richardson in order to make a claim for the money.

Dr Richardson was then called and he recounted his treatment of Nattrass. He had been sent for by Mary Ann, he thought. Because of the symptoms described, he prescribed morphia in an effervescent mixture, but did not attend the patient. He went to see him on the Tuesday and again gave morphia. He was told on Wednesday that Nattrass had had a fit, but Nattrass did not remember it, so, because of the continuing complaint, he prescribed bicarbonate of soda and hydrocyanic acid and carbonate of Lithia. He saw Nattrass every day after that and until his death; on Thursday, he had changed the medicines to morphia and acetate of lead. In the final two days before his death, Nattrass appeared to be getting better and he thought he would recover. He had never witnessed Nattrass having a fit and did not believe he had them. He could see nothing to account for them. He finished with a strange statement:

> The symptoms I observed were consistent with arsenical poisoning and were such as would be produced by the administration of arsenic. I prescribed no arsenic.

This was an extraordinary testimony. If he had observed signs consistent with arsenical poisoning, why did he give George Hedley a death certificate stating death from natural causes? The last sentence, no doubt, is Dr Richardson absolving himself from any blame for the death.

Dr Kilburn gave his deposition, which we noted earlier, confirming his presence at the exhumation of Nattrass's body, the removal of the contents of the viscera, which were then sent to Dr Scattergood. Dr Scattergood then gave his deposition, which confirmed the report examined earlier. He then stated in open court what he had written in his report:

> I examined the earth from the Graveyard, it contained no arsenic whatever. From the appearance which I observed and from the result of the analysis I have no doubt the deceased died from poisoning by arsenic. I give that opinion with great confidence. I

could not, judging from what I observed whether the poisoning was by one or more doses.

Throughout the hearing, Mary Ann had been asked if she wanted to question the witnesses and had refused. Now the charge was read to her that, on 1 April 1872, she did 'feloniously, wilfully and of malice aforethought, kill and murder one Joseph Nattrass'. The charge sheet records that when asked to speak, Mary Ann replied, 'I have nothing to say at present.' The court record states she did not call any witnesses but, when asked if she had any witnesses who should be bound over for her defence, she said she had three: Jane Hedley, George Hedley and Elijah Atkinson. Superintendent Henderson pointed out that these were already witness for the prosecution, and Trotter deliberated if they could be bound over if they were not examined. Colonel Hall asked Mary Ann if she was going to call them now and she replied again, 'no'.

Mary Ann, having no representation and having been ill-advised by Smith, her solicitor, was at the mercy of the system. She knew nothing of legal procedure and the ramifications of not calling witnesses to be examined. Regardless of all that, she now stood committed to trial for two murders.

Before proceedings ended, Trotter informed the Bench that he wished to open the proceedings on the two other cases that would be heard. He wanted to call Jane Hedley again because she was not in good health and he did not wish her to have to return the following Tuesday. He therefore opened the cases of Frederick Cotton junior and Robert Robson Cotton, with the charge that Mary Ann had murdered both.

Jane Hedley's account was brief. She simply gave a few details of the illness of Robert Robson Cotton, his age and the fact that Dr Kilburn had attended. She also said that the symptoms of the illnesses of Joseph Nattrass, Robert Robson Cotton, and Frederick Cotton 'were much alike' and 'the prisoner alone attended on them'. With that, the proceedings were ended until the following Tuesday.

Mary Ann had been taken by Superintendent Henderson to the Sun Inn for a meal at midday. The owner of this inn would be involved in raising money for her defence. (The Sun Inn was eventually demolished brick by brick and rebuilt at the Beamish Museum, where visitors can still see how it looked in Mary Ann's day and enjoy its hospitality). At 6.15 pm Mary Ann, along with her baby, the warden and matron, boarded the train back to Durham.

Mary Ann would have spent the weekend considering her plight. She had sat through two hearings now and had heard her neighbours and friends tell their stories, which she must have realised placed her in a very bad light. For the next three days, as she remained in Durham Goal, she would have been much occupied with the knowledge that on Tuesday, it would all begin again.

Tuesday, 25 February was a terrible day for weather. A snow storm had swept into the Durham area from the north. The preparations for Mary Ann to travel to Bishop Auckland went ahead. The warder and the Matron accompanied her as before; her baby was well wrapped up in her shawl. The train journey allowed Mary Ann to see the snow covered countryside and the bleak pit villages in the distance. Her thoughts would have been fixed on the day ahead and she knew the retelling of the deaths of two children, especially her 14-month-old son, would not be pleasant. Once again on her arrival at Bishop Auckland, she would have to make the bus ride to the court through a crowd who had turned out to stare and point at this so-called monster.

The scene in the courthouse was the same as the previous Friday, with noticeably more people in the 'second class' section. When the proceedings started, the fact that Mary Ann was still without representation was raised. The magistrates, Colonel Hall, Dr John Jobson and Major Hodgson were on the Bench. It was stated that Mr Smith had been appointed as her solicitor and had been seen outside the court but was now not present. Trotter informed the court that monies had been raised from the sale of the prisoner's goods and taken by Smith; Trotter, in his favour, said it was preferred that she should be represented because of the legal arguments and technicalities involved. Colonel Hall said that if Smith had been paid then he should be there. Thompson Smith, the warder, said that Smith had received about £20 from the prisoner and was disappointed he had not been at the hearing on Friday; Mary Ann, however, had made no complaint. Smith had been at the August hearing taking notes, but it was not clear what he had used the money for. The Bench ordered him to be brought to court. The court was informed that

Mr Charles Russell Q.C. would be the leading counsel for the prosecution at the Durham Assizes and Colonel Hall assured Mary Ann that defence counsel for this case would be assigned to her at Durham.

The beginning of the trial demonstrates clearly that Mary Ann did not get a fair hearing in the committals. Smith and Chapman had acted disgracefully; not only did they take her money and let her down, but they actually seemed to be against her. The newspapers would make much of this and history shows these two as charlatans.

The hearing then commenced properly. The first case to be considered was that of Frederick Cotton junior. Trotter named the child and gave his date of death and his relationship to Mary Ann, as step-son.

Sarah Smith was called first. She confirmed she was a near neighbour of Mary Ann's and had known her since her arrival in West Auckland, about four months before her husband Frederick Cotton senior had died. She told the court that Mary Ann had arrived with her husband and three children, a step-son called Frederick, another step-son called Charles Edward and her own son called Robert Robson. She remembered Frederick taking very ill and dying. 'He died', she said, 'on a Sunday in the fore part of March'. A week before he had died, she had been in the prisoner's house, had seen the boy lying on the sofa, and asked if he was not very well. The prisoner had said that he was, indeed, unwell. Smith said she had gone back to the house the next day after the prisoner had sent for her. The boy was still on the sofa and she said he looked very sick and faint. She asked the prisoner what the boy was complaining of and she was told that it was a 'pain in the bowels and bad all over'. Mary Ann had said she hoped he was not suffering from the smallpox. Smith reported that the boy retched but did not vomit and was very sickly. She advised the prisoner to send for the doctor and she said she had already done so. The next day Smith went again to the prisoner's house and the boy was in bed and much worse. The prisoner was trying to stop the bleeding from a leech wound at the right side of his bowels. The boy was sick, vomited and complained of thirst. She reported something that would be commented on by other witnesses:

The prisoner gave him drinks and he very often vomited after the drink. The drinks were given out of a teapot but I do not know what they were composed of.

She continued to tell of Dr Kilburn's assistant Dr Chalmers attending the boy and stopping the bleeding from the leech wound. The boy was purged. He complained of pain in his stomach and bowels frequently. She confirmed she was present when he died, five minutes before 12 o'clock on the Sunday night. She then gave the details that Trotter would want to hear:

> The prisoner attended the deceased throughout his illness, she gave him drinks and I saw her give him tea and toast but he could not eat the toast. No one but the prisoner did anything for the deceased that I saw.

She then made a point about the boy asking for his Glengarry cap to be put on his head when he died. She had helped put the boy in the coffin and had put the cap on his head. (This cap would be used as part of recognising the body at the exhumation). She then told the court that Jane Hedley had brought a fruit loaf on the Saturday night before the boy died. She said that the boy was very sick on the Sunday morning and, after he had died, Mary Ann had ordered some tea and a piece of the fruit loaf was cut off. She ended by telling the court that Mary Ann had asked for Mr Atkinson to come and pray with the boy, which he did.

Phoebe Robson then gave her testimony. She confirmed again that she was a neighbour of the prisoner. She also stated that up to Easter the previous year she had 'lived under the same roof with prisoner in Johnson Terrace'. She gave a similar account of the boy's illness as Sarah Smith. She had asked the prisoner what was the matter with the boy and was told by the prisoner that he had gastric fever. Her testimony then includes the opinion that only Mary Ann attended the boy:

> I did not see the prisoner or anyone else give the deceased anything to eat or drink. The prisoner was always in attendance on the deceased. I saw brandy and two teapots one on the bed head and one on the chimney piece.

She then confirmed the detail of having some of the fruit loaf with the prisoner after the boy died. She also mentioned the Glengarry cap being placed on the boy's head. She finished by commenting that 'no food had been prepared for the deceased'.

Jane Hedley was in the court, despite it being said she would not attend. Her statement was to confirm that she was asked by the prisoner to get a spiced fruit loaf from Bishop Auckland. She cryptically adds, 'She [the prisoner] did not say for what purpose.'

Elizabeth Atkinson was next, and confirmed she was a neighbour of the prisoner. She told the court she remembered the illness and death of Frederick Cotton junior. She said she was in the house on the Wednesday previous to his death. She had asked the boy in the prisoner's presence if he could take anything, to which he did not answer. He then asked her where her husband was and said he wanted him to pray with him. She told how she went home and made some rice milk and sent it to the prisoner's house. She herself did not return to the house until the Saturday. The prisoner was present and Atkinson asked the boy how he was. The prisoner replied that he had had a very restless night. Atkinson again asked the boy if he could take anything and he said 'yes'. She said she went home, prepared some beef tea and took it back to the prisoner's house.

> Mrs Cotton was still there. I put the beef tea on the table. The deceased said 'Thank you Mrs Atkinson' The prisoner then said he was not to have it and I remarked 'well it is an untimely hour'. I felt grieved and came out.

She then told the court that on one of her visits she asked the prisoner if the boy could take anything and she said 'it would do him no good'. Then she gave the detail that was consistent with the other witnesses:

> I laid the deceased out and saw him coffined. He was with his Glengarry cap on. I noticed two teapots in the room, one on the mantel piece. I know the teapots were in use and the prisoner used to give drinks out of them.

It was at this point the solicitor's clerk, Smith, was brought in. He made his brief statement to the court that the money raised had been used for the Nattrass case only. The Chairman of the Bench was exasperated with Smith. He responded to Smith's statement sharply asking if it was not also to 'watch' the current case. Smith gave a one word reply, 'no'.

Kilburn was sworn in to give his testimony. He confirmed that he was called in on 4 March 1872 to see Frederick Cotton junior. He noted him to be a boy of about 10 years old. He said he had been ill for a few days and complaining of pain in his bowels that was increased with pressure. He had been vomiting, which the prisoner told him had not been excessive.

> There was some thirst and anxiety of countenance, his tongue was dry and glazed, I treated him for enteric fever. Leeches were applied and I ordered a mixture containing bismuth, bicarbonate of potash and a few minims of hydrocyanic acid.

He returned to the house on 6 March where he found the boy continuing to have troubles with sickness, but there was not much purging. He ordered a blister to be put on the boy's stomach (A blister poultice was an application used by Victorian doctors to cause a blister to appear on the skin. They believed this would relieve the patient's symptoms based on an older belief that the body could not have two illnesses at once. Substances such as mustard or pepper were often used. The treatment had no effect.) He said he continued to visit the boy up until his death on Sunday, 10 March. He protected himself from accusations of culpability for any arsenic poisoning:

> There was no arsenic or preparation of arsenic in any of the medicines I gave him.

He then turned to the exhumation of the boy's body at St Helen's Churchyard on 15 October 1872. He described the soil as of an alluvial nature and moist. The coffin was in a good state of preservation. When the coffin was opened he saw a Glengarry cap on the head. He described the taking of the viscera and the bottling and sealing of the samples. He confirmed he had given these to Sergeant Hutchinson. He would also confirm he had sent soil samples to Leeds. It appears that on this occasion he had gone to Leeds to be present at the examination of the samples by

Dr Scattergood. He ended his statement by confirming the new cause of death:

> From the post mortem examination and the examination I made at Leeds, I am strongly of the opinion that there were symptoms of arsenical poisoning and I did not see any of the appearances that would have issued from enteric fever but I did not examine that portion of the small intestine that would give indication of enteric fever.

It is a strange statement from a medical expert who claims no evidence of the original cause of death and yet admits not examining that part of the intestine where such evidence might best be found.

Archibald Chalmers then gave his statement to confirm he had not prescribed any medicine and had made up the medicine prescribed by Kilburn. He states:

> There was no arsenic in the medicines I considered he was suffering from gastric fever; if it had been gastric fever the remedies that were prescribed should have relieved it but they had no effect at all.

Thomas Hutchinson followed to confirm he was present at the exhumation of Frederick Cotton junior's body. He stated that there was a coffin plate that bore the inscription:

> Frederick Cotton, died 10 March 1872 aged 10 years.

He also spoke of the Glengarry cap being on the deceased's head. He confirmed witnessing Dr Kilburn remove the viscera and bottling the samples in jars and between plates. He had kept them under lock and key and took them to Dr Scattergood the following day.

Kilburn was recalled and was ask to confirm the exhumation was of Frederick Cotton junior. He swore that the body exhumed was that of Frederick Cotton junior.

Thomas Scattergood's statement was the centre-piece of the prosecution's case. He gave his usual qualifications and confirmed

Hutchinson had handed him the various samples from Kilburn, which he had itemised. The stomach and intestines were the only parts of the viscera that showed inflammation. He repeated the details of his report:

I examined the small intestines most carefully for any of the appearances which are seen in cases of enteric fever and there were no such appearances whatsoever. I analysed the whole of the viscera and found arsenic in all of them in the stomach and bowels with their contents there was about a grain and six-hundredths of a grain dissolved and absorbed and about one eightieth of a grain undissolved. I estimated the quantity contained in the solid organs … at about four tenths of a grain, making altogether a grain and a half.

He went on to say there was no arsenic in the soil he analysed. He concluded that based on his analysis, Frederick Cotton junior had died from arsenic poisoning.

An interesting witness was Thomas Detchon. There is a question as to how he has become involved in the case. There is no connection between Mary Ann in West Auckland and Detchon from Newcastle, which is quite a distance away. There is no way the police could connect him to Mary Ann. It can only be suggested that he initiated contact with the police. Detchon was an assistant in a chemist shop in Newcastle and he was considered a key for the prosecution in trying to establish Mary Ann as a serial poisoner. He testified that on 21 January 1869, a woman purchased arsenic soap 'to kill bugs' at the William Owen chemist in Newcastle. He was the person who served her. He tried to persuade her to buy another product, 'bug specific', but she had insisted on the arsenic based soap. His written and verbal statements were both adamant that the woman was the prisoner:

I remember a woman coming into my Master's shop on the 21st January 1869 and asking for soft soap and arsenic. She asked for three-pennyworth and gave the name of Mary Ann Booth, the prisoner is that woman. Since then I have seen the prisoner with almost a dozen other women in Durham Goal and I picked her out among all the others as the woman who came for the arsenic.

She initially was refused the arsenic soap as there was no witness to sign his poison book. She left and returned with a witness and the soap was sold. He drew a replica of the poison book entry in his sworn deposition. It showed the name of the purchaser as Mary Ann Booth, with a full signature, and the witness as Elizabeth Robson, with a mark as her signature. It is worth noting that Mary Ann had not taken any active part in the proceedings, never questioning any of the witnesses. Major Hodgson asked a question of Detchon about the cost of the alternative offered and was informed it would have cost sixpence – twice the cost of the requested arsenic soap. It was then that Mary Ann decided to ask a question and a strange one it was:

What time of the day was I there?

To which he replied:

To the best of my recollection, between two or three in the afternoon.
That will do,

...was all that Mary Ann said in response.

Jane Hedley was recalled so that the testimony she had given in the Nattrass hearing could also be recorded into the Frederick Cotton junior hearing: that she had gone to Mary Ann's house to get the pot of arsenic soap.

To reinforce the motive for murder, Trotter now called James Young. He confirmed that he was from Shildon, near West Auckland, and represented the Prudential Insurance Company. He said he knew the prisoner and that Frederick Cotton senior, Frederick Cotton junior, Robert Robson Cotton and Charles Edward Cotton were all insured in his office. He had received notice of the death of Frederick Cotton junior and had paid out £5 15s, for which he received a receipt. Again no questions were asked of Young about how these policies were taken out. It was common practice for men like Young to go from door to door in working communities to sign up new business. For a small weekly amount, mothers and fathers could take out insurances to cover the cost of deaths in the house. If he had been asked, he would have testified that almost everybody else along Mary Ann's street had taken out similar polices.

The chairman of the Bench then asked Mary Ann if she wished to call any witnesses, to which she replied, 'No sir. Not at present'. The clerk then read out the charge of the wilful murder of Frederick Cotton junior and Mary Ann was asked if she wished to say anything. After a simple 'No sir' from Mary Ann, she was committed to trial at Durham assizes and the hearing was adjourned.

The next hearing was opened immediately. It was to enquire into the death of Robert Robson Cotton, Mary Ann's own child to Frederick Cotton, who died on 28 March 1872. Jane Hedley had already testified that the child was ill for about a week before his death. It was therefore Sarah Smith who was called first. She began with the usual statements of who she was and then spoke of the young child's illness. She had seen him frequently during his illness.

> He appeared to be very poorly – he was sick and purged, and, as I thought, getting some teeth. During the fore-part of the week he was very poorly, and on the Thursday morning, when I went in he seemed to be a good deal better, and I thought he was all right. I saw him again at dinner time the same day. I thought at dinner time he was all right and I said to Mrs Cotton 'Robbie is all right now' He had a piece of bread in his hand which he was dipping into some kind of syrup. Prisoner said she thought he was all right.

She then recounted how she had returned that night to find the boy in his cradle, with Nattrass ill in the bed in the same room. She looked at the child and described him as giving a 'heavy fetch' ['fetch' was used here as a term for gasping for air and often associated with the noises and action of vomiting, without any vomit]:

> I thought he was dying, it gave such heavy fetches, and there was so long a time between them. Its eyes were fixed. I said to Mrs Cotton 'the child is dying'. Who must I fetch in?' and she said 'Nobody'. I said to Mrs Cotton 'What time did this change take place?' and she gave an answer I did not hear. I then asked her again who I must fetch in, and then she said I might go for the doctor; she mentioned no particular doctor, and I went to Mr Kilburn's surgery.

When she returned, Mary Tate and Jane Hedley were with Mary Ann in the room. She asked Mary Tate if the child was still alive, to which she replied:

'Yes. Did you ever see such a change as this?' I said 'I never did' I then said to the prisoner, 'What have you been giving the child?' She said 'Nothing but a spoonful of soothing syrup'.

At this point Dr Chalmers came in and examined the boy and Smith spoke of Mary Ann having a brief 'fit'. When the doctor had gone, Mary Ann had asked Smith to take the child out of the cradle. The prisoner had asked her if she was frightened of it and if she was, Mary Ann would take the child out herself. Smith did take the child onto her knee and held him for about an hour. She asked Mrs Tate to time the fetches and they were about fifteen minutes apart. She put the child back into the cradle. When he had no more fetches, she knew he was dead and helped to lay him out. Mary Ann then sent her to her sister, Phoebe Robson, to get a nightdress for the boy. She ended her testimony:

During the time the child was ill I was in and out constantly, and never saw anyone Attend to the child except Mrs Cotton. There was no other woman living in the house, and nothing but neighbours like myself going in and out. I can't say I saw her give him anything but the breast.

Phoebe Robson, Sarah Smith's sister, confirmed she had been in and out of the house a few times. Mary Ann had not told her what the matter was with the boy. She said that Mary Ann had asked her to make the child a night dress on the Wednesday night, which was the night before the child died.

Mary Tate then gave her evidence. She stated that she knew both the prisoner and the child, Robert Robson, very well. She had been at the house whilst the child was ill. She said he was poorly for about a fortnight. She continued:

On the Thursday he died, at dinner time he got a good deal better. That afternoon, about two o'clock, I went to my own house, and returned about three. When I went out, I left Mrs Cotton with the deceased. There was no one else in the house but Joe Nattrass, who was ill in bed. When I returned the child was a great deal worse, and I was astonished. I asked Mrs Cotton what was the matter with it. She said 'My child is a great deal worse, Mrs Tate, and don't disturb it.' I asked her if I might bring anyone in. She said 'No, No', the child was dying and I was to let it die quietly.

She stated that she went out to fetch Mrs Smith and then went home. She confirmed that she had been present at dinner time. The child had been standing on Mary Ann's knee when Dr Chalmers came in. She also gave the same testimony as Sarah Smith of the child's last hours and confirmed that when Mary Ann had been asked what she had given the boy, she had replied, 'Only a spoon of soothing syrup'.

Dr Archibald Chalmers was called and confirmed that he had seen the child on the Wednesday before his death. He did not prescribe anything because he believed the child was suffering from teething and was in no danger:

I saw him in the middle of the next day, he being quite well. I saw him again between six and seven, Mrs Smith having come for me. The child was then in convulsions. I remained nearly an hour, but not till he died. He was dying when I left. I did not think the difference in the child between my twelve o'clock and six o'clock visit was extraordinary. It is not unusual in children, who sometimes die before a medical man can be called.

Once again, Jane Hedley was recalled to state on record that she had fetched a pot containing arsenic soap from Mary Ann's house. Then Dr Kilburn was called to the stand again. He had visited the boy on Tuesday, 26 March when he had been suffering from a slight febrile attack caused by teething. He ordered a saline mixture and half a dozen 'grey powders of mercury and chalk'. He had also seen the child on the 28 March:

He seemed completely recovered and was prattling on his mother's knee, the child died on the evening of the same day.

He confirmed the exhumation of the child's body and that he gave Sergeant Hutchinson the samples to be taken to Dr Scattergood. He 'considered they gave evidence of arsenic poisoning'.

Dr Scattergood went through his report as recorded above and confirmed that he had found arsenic in the body parts of between a hundred and twentieth and a hundred and thirtieth of a grain. Again, he was definite in his conclusion that teething was not the cause of death, but that it was as a result of arsenic poisoning.

Thomas Detchon, who worked in the Newcastle chemist's shop, was called again to give similar evidence as before. This time it was Colonel Hall who asked him if he was sure of the time that Mary Ann had purchased the arsenic soap and Detchon confirmed that he was. Hall then asked, 'And you never saw her from 1869 until you picked her out in gaol?' Detchon replied, 'No sir'. Then Hall asked if he had ever seen a photograph of her, to which Detchon answered that he had seen one in the early part of November and that he had seen the prisoner in the gaol in the latter part of that month. Detchon was asked by Hall to swear to recognising the prisoner as the woman who purchased arsenic soap in Newcastle, irrespective of the photograph in the paper. He stated, 'Yes I do'. Hall then asked Mary Ann if she had any questions, to which she replied, 'I have nothing to ask or say at present'.

With this, Mary Ann Cotton was formally committed for trial at Durham Assizes for the wilful murder of Robert Robson Cotton.

The witness Detchon is particularly interesting, in terms of both defence and prosecution. Detchon had seen Mary Ann in prison and identified her there. He also admitted to seeing a photograph of her in the previous November (1872). It was probably seeing that photograph that caused him to contact the police. The defence could have made much more of this. However, there is also other information that the prosecution could have used. The names Mary Ann Booth and Elizabeth Robson were unlikely to have come out of thin air. In 1869, Mary Ann had been married to James Robinson, the shipwright. It was a difficult year for Mary Ann, which would end with her leaving James Robinson. Mary Ann was eventually discovered using James Robinson's money and had been alleged to have been using it for her own pleasures, including going to the races. There is no reason why a woman, looking for a bit of pleasure with ill-gotten money, would not travel to Newcastle for its big-city attraction and well-regarded horse-racing. The argument that it was too far away is unconvincing. As to the names; Mary Ann Booth was the mother of an apprentice to James Robinson (John George Booth) and there was a friend from Mary Ann's childhood, named Elizabeth Walsh, whose mother was called Mary Robson. She lived at Bishopwearmouth in Sunderland. It is possible that the two women had gone for a day out together and that Mary Ann Cotton had used the visit to obtain a substance she did not want to buy locally, particularly if, at that time, she had yet to embark on a career as a poisoner and was plotting how to obtain James Robinson's estate for herself. If two false names were needed urgently, then familiar names would come to mind to serve that purpose.

Notwithstanding this, it must also be noted that a woman calling herself Elizabeth Robson turned up in Newcastle after the trial claiming to be the witness to the poison purchase. She stated that Mary Ann Booth did make the purchase and that it was not Mary Ann Cotton. Elizabeth Robson, however, never produced any evidence as to who Mary Ann Booth really was. There was also no investigation as to who Elizabeth Robson was and if she in fact was Mary Ann's childhood friend. Whatever the case, nothing was done to argue against the evidence of Thomas Detchon.

When reviewing the hearings that Mary Ann Cotton had faced so far, it is useful to step back and examine what happened. In a trial where hanging would be the outcome upon conviction, there must be a certainty that the person is believed guilty, beyond reasonable doubt.

In the hearings so far certain facts are beyond question. We can say that the people who died did so in great agony. All of them were under the constant care of doctors – Mary Ann Cotton had been responsible for calling them in on more than one occasion. She had also, on many occasions, invited neighbours to assist her. Arsenic soap had been purchased by Mary Ann and was found in her home. Mary Ann had used arsenic soap to clean her own house and that of a neighbour. Every death had initially been certified as by natural causes. Subsequently, grains of arsenic, of varying degrees, had been found in the bodies of the deceased.

There are many opinions regarding Mary Ann's behaviour, but nobody definitely saw Mary Ann Cotton giving arsenic to any of the deceased, despite the claims that she was the only one who had attended the deceased prior to death. There are also questions to be asked regarding the evidence of Thomas Detchon – could he really be certain that Mary Ann had bought arsenic soap under a false name some four years previously? What is certain is that there was inadequate legal representation for Mary Ann. No one questioned any of the witnesses; no one challenged the expert opinions and, indeed, no one sought an alternative expert to testify. No one questioned the various doctors or took Kilburn to task about his role, or the initial post-mortem on Charles Edward.

Because of this, we are left with only speculation as to how Mary Ann Cotton fits in with the circumstantial evidence. She was obviously a resourceful woman who had negotiated marriage with four husbands. She was a woman willing to deceive, as evidenced when she stole James Robinson's money and when she married Frederick Cotton bigamously. The reports suggest she was a dominant woman, able to get people to do her bidding. She had a background in nursing where she would have been involved with illness and the doctors who prescribed medicines. Although many neighbours in West Auckland spoke of associating with her and being in and out of her home, none of them seem to have had any intimate knowledge of her or her background before the hearings. This was due to her being mobile and not staying in any one place for too long.

The whole affair with Nattrass and rumours of her involvement with the excise man at the same time, along with her expressions of wanting rid of the burden of her last charge, Charles Edward, do raise suspicions about her behaviour. Then there is the strange 'fit', just as the baby Robert Robson was being seen by a doctor. There was never any record in her history of such fits. Was she just a woman at the end of her tether after four successive deaths? Was this also why she asked the neighbour to take the child out of the cradle and hold it? Or was it all part of the smokescreen drama she was creating to deceive?

Without making any claims as to the guilt or innocence of Mary Ann Cotton, it would appear to any independent minded person, that there was a great deal wrong with these hearings, and more than a shadow of doubt about their conclusions. No doubt some will argue that the point of the hearings was to bring the cases to the Durham Assizes to test the evidence and that is where we now follow Mary Ann.

Chapter 10

The Durham Trial

A s we have already shown, the defence for Mary Ann Cotton was a mess. The letter of help with legal costs from Charles Murray, originally given to George Hedley, had been passed to Lowrey, who had helped Mary Ann by buying her furniture. It ended up in the hands of George Smith. Smith had replied to Murray informing him that defence representation had been organised and instructed. However, the team from Newcastle who were to defend Mary Ann had received no instructions from Smith at Bishop Auckland. The fundraising committee in Bishop Auckland also seemed to fall apart. Thomas Labron, a representative for the committee, went to Durham Goal to speak with Mary Ann. Whatever transpired, we find that on Monday, 3

Sir Thomas Dickson Archibald.

March, Justice Archibald asked Charles Russell which counsel was appearing for the prisoner. His reply is telling:

No, my Lord, the learned counsel who have been mentioned as likely to be instructed have received no communication.

The judge who presided was Canadian born Sir Thomas Dickson Archibald, a trained surgeon who switched careers to become a lawyer.

As we have seen, the Treasury had made the controversial decision to take charge of the prosecution and had appointed Charles Russell. This appointment usurped Durham's own Mr Aspinall and was a difficult one for Mary Ann Cotton. Russell was a Northern Irish Catholic, the brother of a Jesuit priest and three nuns. He had a formidable reputation for extracting the truth and was deemed one of the best lawyers of his day. His annual earnings at the time were, in today's money (2016), around £1 million. Despite all this he was known to be fair and would, in later years, take up the cause of another woman, Florence Maybrick, who was convicted of poisoning her husband with arsenic – this time to protest her innocence.

Justice Archibald requested Mr Thomas Campbell Foster, a Yorkshireman who had not yet taken silk, to represent Mary Ann. He was an able man, very experienced on the Northern Circuit. This was on Monday, 3 March and it was finally decided that the trial would start on 5 March, which meant he had very little time to prepare his case for the defence.

So it was that on 5 March 1873, Mary Ann Cotton made the shortest of journeys, from her cell to the court, adjacent to the prison. She was so notorious by now that hundreds were in the street outside the court and many wanted admission. The Under Sheriff decided to issue tickets and such was the crush in the courtroom that the Grand Jury gallery was commandeered for the ladies of the county. The courtroom was packed to capacity; the great and the good were even prepared to sit on the benches. Outside, those who were not admitted would stand for hours whilst the trial proceeded.

By ten o'clock it was decided to begin the trial and Mary Ann was brought into the courtroom with two wardresses. She was put in position in front of the dock and the crowd strained to get a glimpse of her. One wonders what they expected to see. Would they see the monster of the newspaper reports? What they did see was an ordinary woman, this time without her baby, looking back at them. She was described in later reports as looking pale and old. She had an air of depression and looked heavily weighed down by her situation; her hair no longer tidy and brushed-back as seen in Bishop Auckland. One newspaper report claimed that this was due to Mary Ann's dislike of Thomas Detchon and her fear of him. It reported her as looking haggard; her clothes were less smart and were well worn. She also appeared to need the use of a stick to support her. All in all, she looked a pathetic creature and not the monster they had expected to find. Was this a carefully chosen appearance in an attempt to garner sympathy, or was she finally broken under the weight of her hearings and time in prison?

Charles Russell was supported in the prosecution by Trotter from

Bishop Auckland, Mr Greenhow and Mr Gainford Bruce. Mr Foster had Mr Part to assist him. He had agreed with Russell that the first case to be heard was that of the murder of Charles Edward Cotton, the last of the deaths at West Auckland.

Russell then began and opened his case with a long and challenging address, although he did maintain a fair attitude. He said it had become his painful duty to lay before the jury the facts of the case, as he believed would be proved before them. He was quite sure that the grave and weighty character of the charge of murder against Mary Ann Cotton would receive their earnest attention. He also asked for their unbiased minds to be applied to what they would hear. Aware of the publicity regarding a lack of counsel for Mary Ann, he informed the court and jury that Mr Justice Archibald had requested learned counsel to represent the prisoner. He was sure this would meet with their satisfaction because his learned friend had great experience.

Russell then outlined the charge, 'that the prisoner, on 12 July 1872, at West Auckland, in this county, murdered her step-son, Charles Edward Cotton, and that she murdered him by means of poison'.

He then recounted her time as a widow, by the name of Mowbray, working as a nurse at Sunderland Infirmary. He told of her marriage to George Ward and then to James Robinson and then to Frederick Cotton. He informed the court that they had moved to West Auckland in 1871. The household at the time consisted of Mary Ann Cotton, her husband Frederick, Frederick Cotton junior, Charles Edward Cotton (sons of her husband but not the prisoner), and Robert Robson Cotton, who was her child by Frederick Cotton. He told of her taking in George and William Taylor as lodgers. They had left before the death of Charles Edward. He then very cleverly drew attention to the other deaths by doing exactly that.

In the month of July 1872, the prisoner's household consisted of herself, then a widow, and the sole surviving child, Charles Edward Cotton, the person with whose murder she was charged. I do not propose to call any attention to the details of the deaths of the other members of the family or ask the jury to give them any significance at all.

There is no doubt that this would register as significant in the minds of the jury. He then reminded them again that she was a nurse who could have earned a livelihood, but responsibility for Charles Edward Cotton had prevented her from taking that option. The court was also reminded that Charles Edward was the prisoner's step-son and not her own child. He was a non-earner and did not contribute to the household income and was, therefore, a tie and a burden. He referred back to July 1872 when Mary Ann was in receipt of Poor Law relief for the boy which, for some reason, was due to be removed. He stated that witnesses, although reluctant, would testify that the prisoner frequently complained about the child being a burden. The child was preventing her from working to provide for them and it was a hard situation, because the child was not her own. Russell believed the jury would have no doubt that the child was an inconvenient and embarrassing tie. He insisted 'it would be unjust to say that the evidence would show any systematic and deliberate mistreatment of the boy.' He believed the jury would find that she did her best for the boy, to keep him clean and any failure to feed him was less to do with fault and more to do with her misfortune. However, even though there was 'no systematic cruelty', there would be evidence of frequent acts of cruelty when she badly used the child. There had been great violence entirely disproportionate to the boy's size and she had no love for him. This is a contradiction. Russell had stated she had shown no 'systematic and deliberate mistreatment of the boy' and yet he paints a picture of 'frequent' acts of cruelty. This contradiction was not picked up by Mary Ann's defence.

Russell then turned to indicate a motive for the murder. He informed the court that Charles Edward Cotton was insured by the Prudential Society, for a sum around £8. However, it was not paid out on the boy's death. Russell knew that it was not enough to show that the boy had died from arsenic poisoning, he had to show that Mary Ann Cotton administered it. To this end he told the jury that the boy, 'a little creature of 7 years old', was an apparently healthy and active boy. He informed the court that the prisoner, the boy's step-mother, was the only one who had attended on him. She gave him his food and any medicines prescribed for him. The jury heard that the prisoner called Dr Kilburn in to look at the boy and that he found him ill with symptoms of vomiting and purging.

The wretched life of that little creature', he said, 'ebbed away, and on the 12th of July he died'.

He then stated the charge against the prisoner that she caused the boy's death and caused it by the administration of a deadly poison. The court heard of the circumstances that caused an inquest to be called and of it being held on 13 July. Russell then described for the jury, the post-mortem that Kilburn carried out. He went to great lengths to make excuses for Kilburn's initial conclusion of natural causes. He continually stressed the pressure of time on Kilburn, who had to do the post-mortem just before the inquest. Because he had rushed the job, he was unable to present the inquest with any other verdict than the one of natural causes. Yet, Russell would go on to say, Kilburn had had doubts (he said nothing of the pressure put on him by Riley et al), and carried out the Reinsch test which detected arsenic. Then Russell spoke of sending the viscera to Dr Scattergood in Leeds, which confirmed the presence of arsenic and the conclusion that the child's death was due to arsenic poisoning. If that was the case, then the question was to discover if the poison was accidently or deliberately administered. He believed the jury would conclude, from the evidence, that it was a deliberate act of administration that needed three or four doses. Russell would have liked to bring in the matter of the other deaths at West Auckland, but he knew that this would draw an objection from the defence. As he began to speak on the matter, Foster did rise to object. The judge told Russell that he had done enough and should leave out the details.

The jury, Russell continued, would then have to ask by whose hand the poison was delivered and why. Russell addressed the fact that the evidence would be circumstantial and that it would show that the crime was not one of violence, committed on an impulse of passion, where there would be direct evidence. This, he suggested, was a crime carried out with planning and in secrecy. If there were no direct evidence available, he asked the jury, what evidence would they expect to find? Russell provided the answer: someone who had both the opportunity and the means to get the poison. He had already argued that the prisoner was the only one who cared for, and had access to, the child during his illness. He admitted that when the police examined everything they had found in the prisoner's home, they could find no trace of any arsenic. He advised the jury that if this fact in any way shed a favourable light on the prisoner's innocence and left a doubt with them, they should give it the fullest consideration it deserved.

This advice was quickly followed by Russell telling the jury that the child himself had been sent to the local chemist to buy arsenic soap. The chemist had refused to serve him and so Mary Ann Dodds went to get it for Mary Ann. He told them that the prisoner had required it for cleaning and the killing of bugs. He therefore argued the prisoner had access to arsenic and described how it could be obtained from the arsenic soap. Russell accepted this was speculation, so he turned to motive. In this he spoke again of the insurance money as being the pecuniary interest Mary Ann Cotton had in the child's death. He ended his opening remarks by advising the jury to carefully study the evidence and that, if they had any reasonable doubts, they should find in favour of the prisoner. However, if they believed the prisoner *had* carried out the poisoning, they should discharge their solemn duty under oath and find the prisoner guilty.

Russell's presentation was a master-class in how to set out a case even before the evidence had been heard. He had shown that Mary Ann had opportunity, means and access to the boy and had a pecuniary motive. He also pre-empted any questions on the post-mortem and inquest's conclusion of natural causes. Even the attempt to bring in evidence of other deaths was clever. Foster's objection would suggest to the jury there was something to hide. Russell began to call his witnesses, the first of whom was Isabella Smith.

Isabella Smith stated she was the wife of Samuel Smith, a fireman, and they lived in South Hetton. She had worked at the Sunderland Infirmary until about 1865 or 1866, when she left to get married. She told the court that the prisoner, then known as Mowbray, came to the infirmary to replace her and stayed for eleven or twelve months. During that time she had looked after a patient, George Ward, and eventually married him. Two or three years after Smith had left the infirmary she went back to the new infirmary and saw the prisoner there, using the name Robinson. Some newspapers reported that Smith had used the name 'Robson' (her maiden name) not 'Robinson' (her name when married to James Robinson). Foster cross-examined her and she said that she had worked at the infirmary for twenty-six years. She described how medicines were prescribed and left in the surgery where nurses could pick them up even when surgeons were not present. She added:

> I acquired no scientific knowledge during the twenty-six years I was there. I knew calomel – it was white; but I never meddled with the bottles. I wasn't much of a scholar. A scholar would know poison, as the name was on the bottles.

Sarah Smith, the neighbour who had testified at Bishop Auckland, now came to the stand. She recounted much of what she had said at the Bishop Auckland hearing. She brought in the deaths of the other members of the family in response to questioning by Gainford Bruce. Despite an objection by Foster, this was permitted. Foster was irritated that details irrelevant to the Charles Edward Cotton case were being brought in. Even the death of Joseph Nattrass was mentioned. Smith reinforced the fact that the prisoner was the only one in the house looking after the sick: 'no one else was in the house or lived in it then'. She described how Charles Edward had been ill and vomiting all the time. She then linked the death of Charles Edward to that of his brother, Frederick junior:

> I said to the prisoner that he was very ill like his little brother Freddy. I had been in the house during the illness of Frederick. I didn't stay long in the house. When I told the prisoner that, she said, 'Yes, they were both alike, and both in one way.'

Russell asked her if she had seen the prisoner do anything to the child, to which Foster objected. The judge upheld the objection, 'but if Russell made a point of it, he would consider it'. Foster cross-examined Smith who admitted that she had not lived with the prisoner. She also stated that she had never heard of anyone else living with her either. She also remarked that a good deal of gossip went on in West Auckland and many would gossip about other people's concerns. Re-examined again by Russell, she explained that she had lived six doors away from the prisoner before she moved to Front Street. She had not been in the house more than once before the illness. When she visited, she said she had seen no one but the prisoner and Charles Edward.

Mary Ann Dodds, the neighbour and cleaner for the prisoner, was then called. She stated how long she had known the prisoner and that she had lived next door to her in Johnson Terrace. Under examination by Greenhow, she said that she went to the Front Street home on 8 July, before Charles Edward's death, to clean. She said the boy was not downstairs and was told that he had taken ill on Sunday, 7 July. She described the boy as:

> …a particularly fine little boy for going errands and that. He was active and healthy when I saw him last before this, on the 6th – Saturday night.

She stated no one else was in the house other than the prisoner and Charles Edward. The prisoner invited her to go and see the boy at about 10 o'clock. At dinner time she said that Dr Chalmers, Kilburn's assistant, who Mary Ann had called in, had come to look at the boy. He prescribed medicines, which she went and fetched from the surgery and gave them to the prisoner. They consisted of a bottle and a few powders. She recounted how she had visited Mary Ann on the next two days, but not the Thursday, the day before the boy died. On the Tuesday she had tried to speak to him but he went to sleep. On the Wednesday she had also seen him asleep. She told the prisoner that 'if he kept much longer at this, he would not live much longer'. When she was called to the house on Friday morning, 12 July, the boy was on the sofa and the prisoner told her he had died at about ten minutes to six. She also said he had had convulsions at about midnight. The prisoner told her she thought he had died from gastric fever. Dodds then described how she had washed and laid out the body of the boy and, whilst doing so, found a napkin with 'a motion' in it, which she gave to Dr Kilburn. She then spoke of a conversation she had with the prisoner before the child had died. Dodds had asked her if she was going to send the child to the workhouse, to which the prisoner had said 'no' and that she would rather keep it. The prisoner told her they were going to take the Parish Relief away and 'it would be very hard to keep it for nothing'. Dodds said she had used the arsenic soap to clean the bedstead about six weeks before the boy died. She also spoke of a conversation about 'Mr Mann', the custom and excise officer. She had asked the prisoner if he would marry her if it were not for the boy. The prisoner told her that Mr Mann liked the boy and that he 'adored the ground he walked on'. Under examination, she recounted the story of the boy being sent for arsenic soap and how, after he was refused, she had collected it. It was used by her to rub the bedstead for the bugs that were on the bed. There was a small piece remaining which she left in a lumber room.

Under cross-examination by Foster, Mrs Dodds said that the prisoner seemed kind to the boy. Russell interposed to get her to agree that it was cruel and unfeeling to move the boy from the bed to the sofa. Foster responded by getting her to state that the child was well covered with bedclothes on the sofa. Dodds also confirmed that it was the prisoner who actively called the doctor in on the Monday and two of them were there on the day he died. A question was raised about the child being given a physic (a preparation to stimulate a bowel movement) and Mrs Dodds said she had not done it. She was again asked about Mr Mann. She had heard that Mr Mann would marry Mary Ann if it was not for the boy. She said:

I heard it was a flying rumour, and wanted to know if it was true. After that I didn't believe the report was true. It made no odds to me.

She then described the house as having carpets and being papered with green wallpaper. She described it as 'green with a stone coloured body'. She had applied arsenic soap to the metal bedstead and to the wallpaper. Her descriptions caused some laughter in court. She confirmed the prisoner's house was a clean house. She was re-examined by Russell and stated that:

I gave the child nothing, neither food nor physic. So far as I know and saw, the prisoner was the only person who gave him any. I saw the little boy on the Saturday; he came to our house, and he seemed lively. I never heard the prisoner say that the boy had ringworms.

John Walton Townsend, the owner of the chemist in West Auckland, now gave his evidence. He told of how the boy, he did not know his name at the time, had come to his shop for arsenic soap and had been refused. Mrs

Dodd had then come in five or ten minutes later and bought it for Mrs Cotton. He stated that he had put a half to one ounce of arsenic in the soap. The quantity was important, as half an ounce contained 240 grains and an ounce about 480 grains. Foster challenged his recollection and Townsend admitted that he had told the magistrates at Bishop Auckland that he had used four to six drachms. Foster handed him a transcript of the hearing and asked him to read what he had said:

I told the magistrates to the best of my recollection four to six drachms.

This was important because of the difference in quantity, the latter being only four to six grains. Re-examined by Russell, he still maintained he gave a half to one ounce of arsenic. He explained it had been late in the afternoon, near closing time, and that he had jotted the detail down in his notebook, which he then produced. He stated that he had put the arsenic on the soap and that his son had mixed it. He also stated that his chemist was not the nearest to Mrs Cotton, which was really irrelevant because the shop he owned was just across the street from Mary Ann's house. It was an obvious attempt to suggest she had been avoiding a nearer shop.

Greenhow now examined Thomas Riley, who stated his position as assistant overseer, grocer and draper in West Auckland. He informed the court that he thought he had seen the prisoner on Saturday, 6 July, when he had asked her to look after a smallpox patient. She had refused because she had the boy to look after and could not leave. He claimed she had said she was 'tied by him'. It was at that point she had asked whether the boy could be put in the workhouse, but Riley had told her that she would have to go in with him. He told the court that she said she had written to ask an uncle in Ipswich to take the boy, but he had refused. He said that she expressed the notion that it was 'a great hardship to be taxed by the boy in keeping her from getting a respectable lodger'. She had apparently said the boy was 'nothing to her'. Riley said they had discussed Mr Mann as he had heard the gossip and asked her if it was true that Mr Mann was going to marry her. He gave her reply: 'It might be so, but the boy was in the way'. He reinforced this by saying that the boy was at his right hand as she continued:

118

'It may not make much matter; she would not be troubled long; he would go like all the rest of the Cotton family'. I said, 'you don't mean to tell me this fine healthy little fellow is going to die?' I think her reply was, 'He won't get up'. I thought she meant he would not grow up to manhood.

He then spoke about the Friday following when, as he was passing the prisoner's house, he saw her standing at her front door. She appeared to be in trouble. He asked what the matter was and was told that her boy was dead. He was invited to go into the house but he refused. He said he was surprised and went and told the police at once.

In cross-examination by Foster, Riley accepted that there was a lot of gossip in the village, but that he had never come across anyone not willing to look after their husband's relatives.

Richard William Parr now gave evidence. He was one of the relieving officers of the Bishop Auckland Union. He confirmed that he was paying the prisoner 1s 6d per week. He had last seen her on 6 July (six days before the boy's death) and she had said that the boy was a great inconvenience to her and had wanted him to go into the workhouse. He could not order that. He reported the prisoner as saying that she could earn ten or twelve shillings a week and that the child was not hers to support. He said the boy had looked well, in health and very active. When asked by the judge, Parr said that he had not told the prisoner that the payment was to be her last. When cross-examined by Foster, he stated that he had had no directions to discontinue the payments.

Mary Tate was next. It was obvious when she began her evidence that she was very much changed in her attitude to Mary Ann. She was far more aggressive and hostile. She said she had gone to the prisoner's house on Easter Sunday. (It may be helpful for the reader to know Mary Ann's situation on Easter Sunday. She had buried her baby that day and had Joseph Nattrass very ill in bed. Her older boy had died three weeks before. It can, therefore, be understood that she was under great stress when Tate visited.) She said that she had seen the prisoner strike the boy with her hand. She said the lad was crying for an orange that Mrs Smith had given him,

I went down to Mrs Cotton's house, and the little boy was crying for an orange that Mrs Smith had gave him. I told her to be canny with the child and she said it was her own. The prisoner took the orange from her pocket and put it on the fire, saying the child should not have it. She took the child and hit it with a leather strap. She thrashed him very much.

She stated that she had then gone up to see the ill lodger, Joseph Nattrass. She claimed that Mary Ann would not give the boy enough food, saying it would not bide much in his stomach. She then claimed Mary Ann had said that she had been in Newcastle seeing her husband's brother and, if it had not been for the children, she could have made a comfortable home by marrying her husband's brother. This all seems far-fetched and little more than another rumour, much like the rumour of Mr Mann wanting to marry her. Besides, only Charles Edward was with her at that time and surely a brother would welcome his nephew. We also know, from a letter he had written, that her husband's brother was in London at that time.

In his cross-examination, Foster challenged the truth of Mary Tate's evidence. She retorted that she 'talked about nobody's affairs till she was put to it'. She said that she had told the magistrates at Bishop Auckland about the boy being beaten with a strap, 'I swear that' she claimed. Her deposition from Bishop Auckland was handed to the judge and he pointed out to her that she had not mentioned a strap. She was obviously flustered and blurted out about her own boy crying when 'he wants his whips'. She then said that the prisoner had used the flat of her hand and hit him on the head and face and pulled him by the hair, 'I can't tell you how often I have spoken of this'.

When she was re-examined by Russell she claimed that she had no quarrel with the prisoner, but stated that she 'would not like to whip one of her children as the prisoner did'. She claimed that the strap was one that belonged to the lodger, with a buckle, such as pitmen wear.

The court adjourned for luncheon at this point.

William Davison was the first to be called after the recess. He said he had known the prisoner for about two years and knew the step-son also. He described him as 'a very white boy', but that he was active enough. He said he saw the prisoner beat the boy on 6 July, the Saturday before his death. He said the prisoner had used a double belt made of leather. He told the court she had stopped and then started again. When he was re-examined by Foster, he called the leather belt a 'taws', saying it was a really useful thing and was often used in the Durham area.

John Cary Hendy, a managing clerk in Mr Trotter's office, was then called. He stated that he was present when the previous witness gave his deposition and that the prisoner had been present, but asked no questions. He had also taken down the evidence of Margaret Davison before a magistrate. She was in confinement and could not attend. The deposition was then read to the court. In it, Margaret Davison swore that she had seen the prisoner beat the child and bang his head against the doorpost. It was then that she had shouted to her husband.

Mary Priestly then gave evidence. She was a resident of West Auckland and only knew the prisoner by 'eyesight'. On 6 July, she said she had seen the prisoner calling the boy and when he came to her, she had struck him against the wall. She had also struck him with her foot, according to Priestly, who further stated that the prisoner had locked the boy both in and out of the house for long periods. On cross-examination by Foster, she admitted that she did beat her own five children, 'in the right manner and with a single belt without a buckle. I never take my foot or knee to them.'

James Young's evidence was then heard. He was, as we have already seen from the previous hearings, a representative of the Prudential Insurance Company. He confirmed a number of pay-outs were made to the prisoner. There was an objection by Foster over a signature on one of the papers being produced, but it was eventually withdrawn. He covered much of the information he had already given at the Bishop Auckland hearings, confirming that the life of Charles Edward had been insured with his company and that nothing had been paid out because no death certificate had been produced. He stated that the proposal was signed by Frederick Cotton senior. Under cross-examination, he admitted that a vast number of poorer classes insure in his office, to cover the cost of a decent funeral.

Richard Parr was recalled to state that the costs of Charles Edward's funeral had been borne by the Parish.

Dr Kilburn then took the stand. He was a crucial witness. He had overseen the illness of the child, determined that death was by natural causes, held a post-mortem and presented the results to an inquest as natural causes. While in the witness box, his professional behaviour in this case would be open to public scrutiny.

He began by stating his name and qualifications as a surgeon and stated that he had known the prisoner since her arrival in West Auckland and had attended members of her family before attending the deceased. He had been called into the house on 11 July as he was passing the prisoner's home. He had visited the child twice that day and had prescribed medicines, the first of which the boy vomited, and these were replaced in the evening. He stated that the prisoner was the only one attending the boy. He learned of the boy's death the next day.

> I was asked to make a post-mortem examination. I was startled to hear of the child's death. There was nothing on the Friday to lead me to believe he would die so early.

In this statement, Kilburn was suggesting that it was his surprise at the death that led to the post-mortem, when in fact it was due to the actions of Thomas Riley, which he fails to mention. He confirms that he laid the boy's body on a table in the prisoner's home to conduct the post mortem. He then went through his examination of the body as we have seen above. Kilburn tried to justify his conclusions by saying he was short of time before confirming that the boy died from natural causes. He confirmed that he had not told the inquest at the time that he was under such pressures and that they had determined the death accordingly. Dr Kilburn had been the only medical witness called at the inquest. He stated he had heard that morning that there was green wallpaper in the room but he disagreed, despite the detail given in testimony. He also confirmed that he had buried some of the viscera removed and had replaced the rest back into the body and that he had kept some fluids separately, which he said were in a bottle under lock and key. He then spoke of the Reinsch test he had carried out, failing to mention once again that this was due to pressure from Riley, and discovered arsenic present. He then described the exhumation of the child's body and the sending of samples to Dr Scattergood.

Under cross-examination by Foster, Dr Kilburn agreed that the medicines he and his colleague prescribed were strong poisons and had to be handled carefully. He further agreed that the Reinsch test was objected to by others because of its uncertainty. Foster discussed the test with Kilburn, pointing out that if the acid used was impure it could incorrectly indicate the presence of antimony or arsenic (antimony is a natural occurring metallic element). Foster was aware that Kilburn's finding of arsenic in the viscera was a key point. He knew he had to try and undermine Kilburn's testimony. In pointing out that other doctors had rejected the Reinsch test and by showing how it can be a flawed process, he was sowing the seed of doubt in the jury's minds. Kilburn testily said that his acid was 'quite pure', but did accept that he had not carried out any other test to corroborate the results. Foster pushed him further and asked if the test had showed either antimony or arsenic. By this questioning Foster was attempting to create doubt about Kilburn's evidence.

Mr Justice Archibald intervened and asked, 'Do you mean it was a rough test to as to whether it [the viscera] contained antimony or arsenic?' Kilburn replied 'Yes'. In this cross-examination Foster had, in a way, succeeded, in that Kilburn had moved from claiming the test was a definitive test to accepting it was a 'rough test' for arsenic. Foster was doing his best with the difficult task of defending Mary Ann. Foster then turned to the presence of arsenic in the soil. Whilst it was true that arsenic can be present in soil, Kilburn said he had sent soil samples from the graveyard to Dr Scattergood for examination. However, where the viscera from the boy's body had been buried in his garden, there was a play area for his children and no soil had been tested from this area. Surprisingly Foster did not pursue this, but instead turned to the green wallpaper.

Foster, who had been drafted on to the case at the last minute, and almost certainly reluctantly, made as good a job of it as he could. He took hold of anything positive from the witness. He raised the issues of the arsenic soap used for cleaning and of the green wallpaper in Mary Ann's house, which could have shed elements of arsenic onto the bed, floor or cupboards. He argued that its disturbance could have caused arsenic to be ingested by the boy or caused contamination of food. He asked Kilburn if he knew anything about the arsenical green wallpaper. Instead of a direct answer, Kilburn replied that he had never seen any ill effects from such wallpaper. He did agree, however, that heat could make fumes come off the paper. The judged intervened and Kilburn corrected his answer when asked what temperature caused fumes. Kilburn could 'not exactly say, but did not think a fireplace could do it'.

This demonstrated his ignorance of the matter. In 1857, sixteen years previously, a Birmingham physician, a member of the same medical fraternity as Kilburn, reported suffering from vomiting, abdominal cramps and light headiness each evening, which only ceased when he went to bed. He was in continual pain during these attacks. It was not until he suddenly realised they only happened when he was in his green-wallpapered study (where he sat by the fire to read), that he tested the wallpaper and found that arsenic was the cause of his illness. He stripped the room and the problem went away. He wrote, '…a great deal of slow poisoning is going on in Great Britain'.

Foster pressed further and asked:

Do you know that people have been attacked by chronic arsenical poisoning and some killed by living in rooms covered with paper in which arsenic had been employed?

Kilburn replied:

I have heard so; but I should think it not very likely in these cases. It may cause suffusion of the eyes, irritation of the nostrils, and colic pain about the stomach, but I don't think it would produce death from wallpaper.

This was a questionable argument and another display of ignorance by Kilburn, who had made much of being an expert. *The Lancet*, the respectable medical journal read by most surgeons, had published an account of a 3-year-old boy who had died of arsenic poison. His room was found to be 'layered with arsenic dust'. In 1859, Alfred Hassall, a medical scientist, was sceptical of the idea of green wallpaper being a source of possible poisoning. However, when he conducted an investigation of his own, he concluded that the green paper at the 'cheap end of the market' did create arsenic dust. It is reasonable to assume that the green wallpaper in Mary Ann's West Auckland house would have been from the 'cheap end of the market'. Dodds had testified that, when cleaning the house, she had rubbed arsenic soap into the wallpaper, an action that would cause the arsenic in the paper to flake dust and leech out. Furthermore, Foster pointed out that, because of concerns about the arsenic content, green wallpaper had been banned in Prussia. Kilburn said he had heard of it, which does raise the question as to why he was dismissive of even a possibility that the green wallpaper may be dangerous. The questioning then turned to the arsenic soap.

It seems surprising that more was not made of the green wallpaper. In 1862, only ten years previously, four children in Limehouse, London, died over a short period of time. With symptoms of respiratory problems and sore throats, high temperatures, stomach complaints etc., doctors suspected that diphtheria had killed the children. However, Henry Letheby, a public health officer, discovered that the children's room had green wallpaper with three grams of arsenic per square foot – a lethal dose. These conditions were much like that of Mary Ann's house but, if the green wallpaper was responsible for the poisoning, it may be asked why Mary Ann and Mary Ann Dodds, her cleaner, were not also affected by the ingestion of the arsenic. At the time, many case reports stated that not everybody in a household was affected. It appeared that only those with an 'unfortunate constitution' were overcome.

Foster tried to pursue the matter of the arsenic soap as a cause of the poisoning. The absorption of arsenic by hands immersed in water that contained arsenic soap was considered. This was dismissed by Dr Kilburn, and Foster ended by getting Kilburn to agree that the boy's body bore no signs of any ill-treatment with any marks or bruises.

Russell, in re-examination, went over the medicines prescribed, the green wallpaper, the arsenic soap and Kilburn was happy to agree that none of these were an issue in the death of the boy.

His assistant, Chalmers, took the stand. He went through his care of the child during his illness describing the symptoms and his prescriptions. He said they had not the slightest effect on the boy. The judge asked him about the safety of the poisons in the medicines, to which Chalmers replied that they were quite safe to take, with 'only a few minims of Prussic Acid' being prescribed.

Foster questioned Chalmers about where the poisons were kept in the surgery. They were kept on a separate shelf but among them were arsenic (in both powder and solution), Prussic acid and the like. He was asked how far the arsenic bottle was from the Prussic acid bottle. Chalmers could not say for certain, thinking it was the fourth or fifth bottle. Foster pressed on and asked where the Prussic acid bottle was, and again Chalmers said he was not certain though 'thought it near the end of the shelf, which contained eight or ten bottles in total'. Realising what Foster was driving at, Chalmers was being evasive and conflicting in his evidence. Foster asked about the distractions from patients attending the surgery and Chalmers agreed that there was always someone waiting to be seen. The line of questioning was not taken any further and Chalmers confirmed that Mary Ann had been very anxious to have the boy seen. As far as he could judge, she showed all the kindness and attention that a mother should show.

Russell re-examined Chalmers in order to refute any suggestion that he had made up a prescription wrongly. He made Chalmers state his professional history and experience in making up medicines; 'In fact' he said 'it is my business'. He stated that he had not made any mistakes and that everything he had compounded for the child could not have harmed him.

Thomas Hutchinson was called and stated that he was the sergeant of police at West Auckland. He recounted his visit to the prisoner on 13 July, the day after the child's death. He told her that the doctor was not going to issue a certificate and that an inquest was to be held. When she asked why, he told her the doctors would not issue it. He then stated Mary Ann's response.

She said, 'Oh people are saying that I poisoned him; but I am clear. I made application to Mr Riley and the relieving officer to get him into the workhouse.'

She said that she had written to ask the boy's uncle to take him, but he would not do so. She also told Hutchinson that she had had a good deal of trouble with the Cotton family, so many of them dying in such a short time. She was also reported as saying that she was only his step-mother and had no right to keep him adding, 'He has prevented me from earning many a pound.' Hutchinson also spoke of searching the house with Superintendant Henderson on 18 July and finding some powders and pills. (These were later found to be innocent by Dr Scattergood). He then confirmed that he was at the exhumation, and had taken the samples obtained to Dr Scattergood. On questioning by Foster, he added that he had found some empty medicine bottles and some 'red lead' but nothing else. Re-examined he said that whatever he had put in the parcel had been transferred to Mr Lockwood (Dr Scattergood's assistant).

Dr Kilburn was recalled to confirm that he had not removed any bottles with medicine in them and did not see the parcel made up.

Lockwood was called to confirm receipt of the items from Hutchinson and of passing them onto Dr Scattergood.

Superintendent Henderson briefly stated that he had gone to arrest the prisoner and when he spoke to her, Mary Ann had made no reply. He described the house search and stated only arrowroot, red lead and some pills were found.

The next witness was to be Dr Scattergood, but it was expected that he would need a long time to give his evidence. The case was therefore adjourned at around 5.30 pm.

The court resumed the following day, 6 March 1873. Mary Ann entered the court and was reported to be looking very pale and 'a little feebler'. When the court settled and proceedings began, Russell called Dr Kilburn back to the stand to confirm that the quantity of stomach contents was 40 drachms, which had been placed in a clean bottle before being sent to Dr Scattergood. Foster took the opportunity to question again the positioning of the medicine bottles in Kilburn's surgery. He was asked about the purity of the bismuth he had used and he accepted that he had not analysed the powder to ascertain its purity, (Foster knew that bismuth had, at times, been found to contain arsenic).

Dr Scattergood then took the stand. After stating his qualifications to give expert testimony, he confirmed that Hutchinson had handed the samples from Charles Edward Cotton to Lockwood and he had, in turn, handed them to Scattergood. He also confirmed receiving the items removed from Mary Ann's house and had determined them to be red lead, arrowroot, borax and some pills that contained a vegetable root. No (arsenical) poison was found in any of them. The fluid he had received from Kilburn, he said, contained around half a grain of arsenic. He said he had washed the stomach because it was covered in soil and had found it to be inflamed and red in certain areas. He believed that this was consistent with poisoning. He confirmed that he had also found arsenic in the bowels, liver, heart, lungs and kidneys. Russell asked Scattergood if the administration of the poison was in one dose or over a period of time. Scattergood went through the processes of arsenic's progression through the body and believed the administration was over a period. He dismissed the idea that anything the doctors had prescribed could have caused the death. The quantity administered must have been large in order for the quantity he found to be left behind. His conclusion was definite:

> In my own mind I came to the conclusion that the cause of the death of the child, from appearances I found from analysis, the presence of poison in the stomach and other viscera, I came to the conclusion that the deceased died by poison, by arsenic. That is my clear and undoubted opinion.

Russell then moved to ask Scattergood if he had made three other analyses. At that point, Foster objected. There then followed a discussion on the precedents in law. Foster wanted the jury to be excluded from the arguments but Mr Justice Archibald refused because the matters had already been discussed in the hearings at Bishop Auckland. The debate therefore continued with both Russell and Foster citing cases to support their opinions. Foster quoted the cases of Regina v. Holt, Regina v. Gearing and Regina v. Faidge to support his claim that such evidence was inadmissible and quoted *Taylor on Evidence* in further argument.

Both Russell and the judge referred to Regina v. Garner and Regina v. Geering to contend that the evidence could be heard. The judge listened as the argument went to and fro and then retired from the courtroom to consult with Baron Pollock. Baron Pollock had the status of Queen's Counsel and had recently been knighted and raised to the Exchequer Bench. He was considered one of the greatest lawyers in England and his opinions on court procedure carried great weight. It is hard to overstate the importance of the decision made on the admittance of the evidence from the other three cases; Nattrass, Frederick Cotton junior and the baby Robert Robson Cotton. If the evidence was admitted, Mary Ann would be seen as a serial killer, without the benefit of the three cases being given a full examination in court. This would prejudice Mary Ann's right to a fair trial. (In 1898 steps would be taken to deal with the principal that the prosecution could introduce 'bad character' evidence. As late as 2003 the issue was still being clarified).

After reviewing all the quoted authorities, the decision was made that the evidence should be allowed. This was a devastating blow to Mary Ann's defence. Russell, aware of any claim that the decision was unfair and with an eye to any appeal on that basis, asked the judge if he reserved any question, to which the answer was that he did not. With this Scattergood was recalled and continued his evidence.

Scattergood addressed the issue of arsenic soap and described the procedure necessary to obtain arsenical powder from it. He had carried out such tests on soap similar to that used by the prisoner and obtained six grains of arsenic. Asked by the judge if the taste was similar to soft soap, Scattergood said he did not find any trace of soft soap. The judge again asked if soft soap exposed to the atmosphere became dry. Scattergood agreed that if on a rag it could do so and that arsenic was a dry powder. Scattergood also agreed, when asked by Foster, that green wallpaper did contain large amounts of arsenic and was dangerous. When asked by Foster to explain why, he stated that when the green substance wears off, it falls out as the paper becomes dry and is diffused in the air. It would also come off if the walls were swept or brushed in cleaning. Scattergood agreed that such flaking of the arsenic had caused health problems. When asked by the judge whether he was aware of any deaths from green wallpaper, he replied that 'he had not read of one'.

Again, this demonstrates either the great ignorance of a poison 'expert' or a dissembling by the doctor. As noted above, documented cases were in the public domain, and especially in medical publications.

When pressed by the judge and Foster, Scattergood agreed that arsenic could be present in the room from both the green wallpaper and the arsenic soap drying out on the bedstead. Scattergood insisted that all of this was irrelevant and that his conclusion that the boy died from arsenic poison still stood. Scattergood concluded his testimony by stating that even though bismuth was impure, it would not have any 'injurious effect'.

Phoebe Robson was then called and she repeated her evidence given at Bishop Auckland. She spoke of the illness and deaths of the two step-sons, Frederick junior and Charles Edward, of Mary Ann's son Robert Robson and that of Joseph Nattrass. In the latter case she described, in detail, the horrific agonies that Nattrass had gone through. Again she stated that only the prisoner had waited on Nattrass and on the two boys. Questioned by Foster, she said that had Mrs Tate washed for the prisoner and, during Nattrass's illness, a Mrs McKeiver had done the washing in her own home. She had never seen any washing done in the prisoner's house and did not know whether yellow soap or soft soap was used.

The two Taylor brothers were then examined individually. They confirmed the time they had spent in the prisoner's house as lodgers. In testimony and questioning, by both the prosecution and defence, they gave a picture of Nattrass's death and that of the boys, Frederick junior and Robert Robson. William Taylor spoke of the meals they had shared, made by the prisoner, and of the routine of going to work from the house. He had never seen the prisoner and Nattrass have any arguments. He stated that Mary Ann was kind and attentive to Nattrass. In cross-examination he stated that the two children and Nattrass had taken ill and died within twenty-one days. He said the prisoner washed for them, but he never saw her washing nor did he know of any bugs or arsenic soap being used. William Taylor had left before the death of Charles Edward. He said that Mary Ann had brought in women after Nattrass's death to clean and prepare food – this is contrary to other claims that Mary Ann alone had prepared food and waited on the deceased. He also confirmed that the prisoner had taken employment to look after Mr Mann.

His brother simply spoke of the two children being ill and gave some details of Nattrass's illness. He said the prisoner looked after them when they were ill and that there was no one else to look after them. When questioned, he stated that the prisoner was always kind and attentive to Nattrass and the children. He particularly mentioned the infant Robert Robson and described Mary Ann nursing him and being very fond of him. He said Nattrass had lived very well at the house. He had had his own washing done at the house and had heard no complaints about bugs. He had left the house after Nattrass died and before the death of Charles Edward.

Dr Richardson, who had attended Nattrass during his illness, described the illness and treatment. Nattrass had told the doctor that he was improving and 'felt better' three days before his death. He said that the death was, therefore, a surprise to him. He confirmed that he had certified the death as natural causes. When examined by Foster, Richardson detailed the medicines (morphia and acetate of lead) that he had prescribed for the symptoms, which, in his opinion, arose from gastric or typhoid fever. He said the prisoner had come to him three times for medicines for Nattrass and had asked that he urgently went to see him. He testified:

> During the whole seven times I saw him, he never once said a word against the prisoner, but said words equivalent to that she had been very kind to him. He died and the prisoner lost a good lodger. I understood from the prisoner that he was about to marry her.

Asked by Russell, Richardson said that he was only consulted for the pain Nattrass was suffering. He still believed that Nattrass had Bright's disease of the kidneys. He had certified the death as from typhoid fever with disease of the kidneys. There is confusion here. In his deposition for the Bishop Auckland hearing, he had stated that he believed the cause of death was from arsenic poisoning, yet at Durham he returned to his original cause of death – kidney disease.

Dr Kilburn was then recalled and confirmed that he had had attended the two other children but not Nattrass. He confirmed the certification of each death as natural causes, enteric fever in Frederick junior's case and convulsions from teething in Robert Robson's case. He told of the exhumations of the children and Nattrass and of sending samples to Scattergood. Kilburn stated that the prisoner had been kind to the children and suspected no foul play. He now stated that, as a result of the analysis by Scattergood, he believed the deaths to be caused by arsenic poisoning. He said that he had heard that the prisoner was unwell at that time, but had not heard of any symptoms.

Dr Scattergood was then recalled and went through the cases of Frederick junior, Robert Robson and Nattrass, and gave his opinion that all had died from arsenic poisoning. He stated that he disagreed with the certifications of the other doctors. Kilburn and Chalmers in turn stated that each certification was made because that is what they had believed at the time. Kilburn gave his revised opinion that all three other deaths were indeed caused by arsenic poisoning. Dr Richardson, however, maintained that his certification of Nattrass's death by natural causes was correct.

With that, Russell declared the case for the prosecution closed.

There then followed an important discussion between the judge, the prosecution and the defence.

Mr Justice Archibald intervened. He wanted to clarify what Russell had outlined in the case for the prosecution. He spoke to Russell: 'There was evidence of arsenical poisoning, but not against the prisoner, unless they relied upon the fact that there was no one else there. What evidence was there of possession of poison in the house at this time?'

Russell replied, 'I think a stronger case of circumstantial evidence it is impossible to make out. There is the actual possession of poison.'

This was a crucial point. Russell had argued a case for arsenical poisoning and had brought evidence from witnesses to make his case. What he had not shown was that at the time of Charles Edward Cotton's death, Mary Ann had possessed arsenic. The judge told him that he had only shown that this was the case six weeks before the death of Charles Edward Cotton. Mr Justice Archibald had correctly noted the evidence of the police that no poison was found in their search of Mary Ann's house. Russell, obviously frustrated, said he would call another witness but Foster objected; Russell had closed his case and could not now reopen it. The judge rebuked Russell, telling him, 'If you have any evidence of poison being in possession [of Mary Ann] you ought to have produced it.'

Russell was obviously angry and made a strange response, 'Even to suggest it was doubtful'. It is not clear what Russell meant but it does suggest he was concerned that his case was being undermined. The judge appears to help Russell, 'You rest your case on the fact that she [Mary Ann] is the only one in the house?'

Russell then handed the judge Jane Hedley's deposition, made at the Bishop Auckland hearings. Hedley was in the local hospital having gone into labour and was not present in the courtroom. Here we again see a problem with the legal proceedings. The judge had made clear Russell had closed his case and could not call another witness, yet he is allowed to introduce more evidence.

Whilst the judge was reading, Russell seemed to be rebuking the judge:

If your Lordship had followed me in my opening, you would have seen that I referred to the mode of giving it, and the using it after the death of Nattrass and before the death of the child.

The judge began to speak again and there were a series of interruptions.

The judge:
There is evidence that six weeks before the death of Charles Edward...
Russell: But if there is no evidence at all....
Foster: I have got a note of what my friend said, 'Six weeks before the death of the child', that would be six weeks after the death of these other three persons.

Russell, caught on the back foot, addressed the judge and said he didn't consider it of so vital importance. The judge retorted that was for Russell to consider and declared that the case for the prosecution was closed. Russell had lost the argument.

Foster addressed the judge: 'I shall ask your Lordship to strike out all the evidence as showing no possession of poison previous to the death of Frederick Cotton, Robert Robson Cotton and Nattrass.' Foster was arguing that any evidence of poisoning, in the three cases that had been introduced, should be discounted as there was no evidence that Mary Ann possessed poison. Russell responded by arguing that the possession of poison had 'nothing to do with it'. Using the Gearing case referred to earlier, the judge stated that the detailing of the family history was justified. The judge refused to accept Foster's argument that Scattergood's evidence was not justified purely on the basis of Foster's cross-examinations, which argued for accidental death or death by natural causes for Edward Charles Cotton. The prosecution had the right to show that there had been a series of deaths that were suspicious. Foster knew he had lost the argument in this instance but, in order for it to be included on record, he stated that it had not been shown that the prisoner was in possession of poison when the other three people had died. He then stated he would not be calling any witnesses.

The lack of witnesses for Mary Ann points to the disgraceful legal representation by Smith at Bishop Auckland. He had not, as he could have done, gathered witnesses to testify on Mary Ann's behalf. There were people in West Auckland and from her past who would have spoken of the good aspects of her character. One cannot blame Foster for this; he had been given the brief late and had only two days to peruse the evidence from the hearings at Bishop Auckland. He would have had no time either to research the more detailed evidence on green wallpaper and therefore Mary Ann was left without a fully prepared defence.

With Foster's closing remarks, the case was adjourned until 10 o'clock the following day.

Later on the Friday, it was reported that Mary Ann had great anxieties about the coming day. She was no fool and realised that her defence had not been the best. She was even concerned that the lack of money to pay counsel would affect her day in court. Though reassured this would not be so, her anxieties remained. The case was still a matter of great public interest and, as on the other days, the court was packed by the great and the good as well as ordinary folk. The crowd included the good ladies of Durham, who took particular interest in the hapless woman before them.

The Shields Daily Gazette describes the scene in the courtroom:

She [Mary Ann] again occupied a seat in front of the dock, from which she frequently rose to give instructions to her advocate, but still, although she seemed tolerably firm, her countenance displayed the most unmistakeable traces of the anxiety with which she waited the result of the trial. Her lips quivered several times during the address of Mr Russell, but when Mr Foster began to speak as to the want of motive for the murders, and as to her treatment of her own child, she sobbed, as though she was almost broken-hearted. She speedily calmed herself, however, and afterwards listened attentively to the various points raised in her behalf; but still during the remainder of the day, she manifested symptoms of concern and despair which had not previously been traceable in her features.

Foster began by recalling Mrs Dodds and questioned her about Mary Ann, claiming she had been ill after the death of the boy.

It appeared that Mary Ann had taken ill, complaining of pains in the head and throat, and had sent Mrs Dodds to ask Dr Kilburn to attend. He was not at the surgery so she had asked Chalmers instead. He had said that because Mary Ann was no longer on Poor Relief he wouldn't attend. When questioned about which bed Mary Ann had taken to, Dodds confirmed that it had been the same bed that the boy had been ill in.

Russell began his summary of the prosecution's case. The jury strained forward paying him the closest of attention. His voice was strong and gripping as he emphasised the circumstances of the death of Edward Charles Cotton. He described the story as 'a sad and appalling one' and he wanted to point to some conclusions that he was sure the jury would reach. Russell had a reputation as a QC and it was expected that his address to the jury would be dramatic and forceful; later reports made clear that he did not disappoint his expectant listeners.

He made clear that the appalling crime had been committed by someone. Someone had deliberately administered poison to the child. He said he wanted to be fair to the prisoner and the jury in informing them why the collateral evidence from the previous day was allowed. He said that the law made it clear that, where there were a number of occurrences of a similar nature, occurring apparently under the same conditions, as was the case here, they should all be considered and the court had wisely said the evidence was to be allowed. They had heard, therefore, of the deaths of Frederick Cotton junior, Robert Robson Cotton and Joseph Nattrass. The description of the illnesses was the same, as were the symptoms and indeed their deaths by a common cause. However, he reminded the jury, they were not here to determine the cases of the three previous deaths, they were to consider the charge against the prisoner; that she had deliberately murdered her step-son Charles Edward Cotton, by the administration of poison. He again stated that admitting the evidence of the other deaths was right and that in considering the charge of the murder of Charles Edward Cotton, the jury needed to be aware of those deaths. They should not give too much weight to this, but they must not also give too little weight to it. He was using the evidence to refute the possible claim of death by natural causes, or accidental administration of the poison. He went on to say he would not speak of the past history of Mary Ann but he did need to point out one fact. Isabella Smith had given evidence that the prisoner, then Mrs Mowbray, had some considerable skill as a nurse in the administration of medicines. She would have gained some knowledge, to one degree or another, of the use of medicines and their application and the circumstances in which they applied. The jury, he said, had been made aware that she was also Mrs Ward. He then led them to consider Frederick Cotton senior, who had died three months after arriving in West Auckland. He spoke of the deaths in the household and the lodgers leaving. The dwindling of the once numerous household had to be an important fact for the jury to consider. He said by 6 July, the household was down to two. Russell went on to paint a picture of Mary Ann, the child's step-mother, alone in the house with the 7-year-old boy, a boy she did not want and had tried to have admitted to the workhouse. 'He was a tie upon her, a tie she was willing to get rid of, a tie she had tried to get rid of, but she failed.' He argued that she had shown him no real motherly tenderness in his blighted life. More than one witness had said that Charles Edward was a pale lad, but an active and healthy boy. Russell indeed was dramatic as he added:

Even the joyless character of his life, that seemed never to have been warmed with the sunshine of a mother's love, could not stamp out the spontaneous joyousness that was planted in his breast.

No one in the Victorian jury could not be moved by Russell. He continued to state that on 6 July there was no suggestion of illness of any kind. Again his dramatic language was employed to effect:

On that very day when the prisoner was complaining that the boy could not be taken into the Workhouse, and she was afraid that the Poor Law relief would be stopped, that healthy child took ill, and before seven days had passed that child was dead. His young life was snapped as the blasted and withered blossom on the trees might be.

This was powerful stuff. Russell linked the desire to be rid of the child with his sudden death, which snuffed out his future just as the 'blossom on the trees' had lost their chance to flower.

He turned to Kilburn's evidence and defended Kilburn's initial decision to declare a natural cause of death. Kilburn, he said, was a village surgeon who shrank from deciding foul play as a cause. He had doubts and decided on an analysis that led to the discovery of foul play. (This was not the case. It was Thomas Riley's insistence that caused a re-think, but this was never mentioned). He then informed the jury that they had to decide whether the death was caused by poison. If it was, they had to decide whether the poison had been administered accidently or deliberately. In this matter he referred to the three other deaths and their similarity – except for the baby Robert Robson Cotton. His was a worse case because in the morning he had been healthy, having recovered from a slight teething attack, but by night he had been having convulsions and subsequently died.

He then reviewed Dr Scattergood's evidence and the finding of arsenic in different quantities in the bodies of Frederick Cotton junior (One grain and seven hundredths of arsenic dissolved and one eightieth of a grain undissolved), Robert Robson Cotton (The quantity was small), Joseph Nattrass (seventeen and three quarters of a grain) and Charles Edward Cotton (about two grains). He asserted that these facts confirmed that the deaths were caused by poisoning. Furthermore, he went on, Dr Scattergood had come to the conclusion that the poisoning was by repeated doses administered over a period of time and by the throat. Russell then turned to the question of intentionality. The jury had to decide whether the poison was given deliberately. To this end, he turned to Foster's arguments that the poisoning was by other means.

He referred to the idea of arsenic soap being the cause, but he pointed to Scattergood's opinion of repeated doses. As the boy would have had to take in the soap on a regular basis, this would seem improbable because of the nauseous and unpleasant nature of the soap. He then dismissed the idea of an error in the prescribing of medicines. He quoted Kilburn, Chalmers and Scattergood, who had all dismissed this idea. He spoke of the use of arsenical water used by the boy, through washing and again quoted Scattergood's statement that he had never heard of such a cause of death. Speaking of the idea of the use of arsenic soap used to clean the bed as a possible cause of arsenic in the air and on the floor, where the boy may have dropped his bread, he pointed to Scattergood's conclusion that it did not account for arsenic in the stomach. Russell then posed the question: could accidental poisoning account for the four deaths the jury had heard about? Again he brought to bear his great skill in oratory addressing the jury:

> I am very much mistaken, if I was not now justified in saying that I have made good the words with which I opened this case; that they were to inquire into the history of one of the most dangerous, one of the most appalling, and one of the most atrocious crimes that ever disgraced this country; and that I have made good the charge that the death was by poison deliberately administered.

Thus having invited the jury to agree with his argument, he asked them to consider who had deliberately administered the poison. He told them that they knew from their own experience that no one could be called to give evidence of seeing the poison actually being made up and of witnessing it being given to a person. Such a situation would be unbelievable if someone allowed themselves to witness such a crime 'that made the flesh creep and the blood curdle'. Russell then said if there could be no witness to the actual administration of the poison, then the search had to be for whoever had a motive. Surely, he argued, no one else but the prisoner could have had a motive. In this, he pointed to the insurance on the young boy's life, which he claimed the prisoner had taken out. The judge intervened at this point and reminded the jury that it was the boy's father who had proposed the insurance. Russell argued that Mary Ann had signed the proposal and with no father around the living parent would benefit. With that he turned to Mary Ann's feelings for the child and her conduct towards him. He pointed to the testimony of witnesses who had said she used violence against him and locked him out of the house. He spoke of testimony that showed she felt the boy was a 'tie' on her and that 'she had no mother's kindness of heart towards it'. He told the jury that she had tried to get the child put into the workhouse and had told Mr Riley that he was a 'tie' on her and that he would not 'get up'. Riley had commented that 'this fine little fellow, he appears to be a healthy little fellow', but by that Friday, the boy was gone. Russell again brought the weight of other deaths in. 'He did not get up, but went like the rest of the Cottons, to the astonishment of Drs Kilburn and Mr Chalmers, who never believed his case to be serious.'

Russell said he wanted to dwell on two points before he proceeded. The first was the witnesses who spoke of the prisoner's great anxiety to get medical attention for the child. This was indeed the action expected of an innocent, concerned person. However, it would also be the action of a guilty person trying to divert attention from their criminal activity. He cautioned the jury not to give much weight to this matter. Then he turned to the means of poisoning the child. He argued that it had been shown that, six weeks before the boy's death, arsenic soap had been purchased in West Auckland, where there were many druggists. He referred to 'persons who spoke to the prisoner being at Newcastle', even though this had been evidenced in court. It had also been shown that a person with skill could make arsenic out of the soap. Russell then posed the question as to who would have opportunity to administer the poison to the boy. The household had been reduced to just the prisoner and the child. Could anyone else be guilty?

Russell then addressed the jury and again cautioned them to consider very carefully if there was any reasonable doubt that the prisoner had poisoned the boy. If there was then it was their solemn duty to say so. He told the jury that he and his team had carried out their painful duty to lay the evidence before them. He believed he had been fair, had pointed out the facts and that it was now up to them to consider these facts and decide whether or not they led to the conclusion that the prisoner was guilty beyond any reasonable doubt. Russell intoned he had done his duty, they must now do theirs.

Russell had done, as expected, a first-class job in his pleading of the case. He had laboured the points where guilt was most possible and skimmed over areas where the evidence was thin, for example in countering the arguments about an error in the prescriptions, or of the dust on the bed and carpet. He had signally not mentioned the green wallpaper in his summation. There is no doubt though that he had laid the foundations for Mary Ann Cotton's guilt to be confirmed.

Foster had a mountain to climb. He had come into the case late with no time for adequate preparation and had cross-examined witnesses as best he could. He now had to stand and make a summing up that held

Mary Ann Cotton's life or death in the balance. He was a good man and would do his best as he rose to address the jury.

He argued that if they were to review the whole of the evidence, they would find nothing that showed the prisoner had administered the poison but there was everything to show that it was not in her heart or mind to do so and they must give her the benefit of the doubt. He spoke to the jury of their two long days listening to Russell 'laboriously' going through the case. He acknowledged their tiredness and asked them to consider Russell's case. He too used language to conjure up an image of a flawed case for the prosecution:

> I give credit to my learned friend for the proofs he resorted to, as a lame man resorts to a crutch which he cannot walk without. He used his props, and as he went step by step, he did it laboriously.

He was recognising that the jury must be tired and thus encouraged them to sum up careful attention free from any bias and free from prejudice. He told them that they must only consider the evidence presented by the Crown and the prisoner and ignore the newspapers and rumours that they would have heard. He referred to the admission of the evidence of other deaths and, whilst he would not quarrel with the judge's decision to allow it, it had cast much responsibility on the jury. They now had to question the way it was introduced and why. He queried what relevance the historical facts had on this case. He challenged it and questioned whether it was fair and without prejudice. Mary Ann had not been tried for any other murders and if she had, and been and found guilty, then that history would not have been allowed in evidence. He told the jury that the introduction of her previous marriages to Ward and Mowbray had been used to insinuate into their minds that they too had possibly died by illegal means. The judge intervened and said no insinuation whatsoever had been made with the evidence, and Russell said he was glad to hear the judge say this. However, if no insinuation had been intended, then what had been the point of introducing it? Introducing the deaths of the Cottons and Nattrass, without any guilt admittedly the prisoner in their deaths was unfair, as the prisoner had no opportunity to defend herself in those cases. The evidence that they had died of arsenic poisoning was brought in to prejudice the jury against the prisoner. Foster argued that it was a crutch to help the prosecution with a weak case.

He further argued that the evidence of the Taylor bothers showed that the prisoner had made meals and cared for them and that they saw no evidence of anything untoward. The prosecution had argued that she 'might' have got the poison in West Auckland or somewhere else, yet there was no evidence of this. Foster argued that the case had been in newspapers up and down the country so why hadn't other chemists come forward to testify that they had supplied the prisoner with poison? The prosecution had not shown any evidence of the prisoner being in possession of poison in the case of the previous deaths.

Foster was in a difficult situation because evidence of the other deaths had been introduced. Scattergood had been very clear that their deaths were due to arsenic poisoning. Foster had made attempts to prevent the introduction of this evidence and when that failed, he suggested that they were either accidental or from natural causes. His only course was to show that there was no reason why Mary Ann would want to see the deaths of the three.

He turned to the motives for the previous deaths. Russell, he argued, had promised to show a motive in the death of Charles Edward cotton, but he had produced no evidence of motive for the other deaths.

> If it were necessary to place motive before them [the jury] with regard to Charles Edward Cotton's death, I want to know how far it was necessary to supply motives with regard to Nattrass, Frederick Cotton and Robert Robson Cotton.

Russell objected at this point that he could not have pointed out motives in these cases. This was because the evidence that was allowed was only in regards to the number of suspicious deaths in Mary Ann's house. A fuller presentation of other evidence could only have been made at a trial on each charge of murder. The judge confirmed that no motives had been introduced.

Foster said he did not care whether his learned friend [Russell] did or did not introduce motives. '…if he could have, he would have done so. What motive was there?' Foster continued to show that there were in fact benefits to Mary Ann that were lost upon the death of Nattrass. He was a lodger and like the Taylor's, had paid his way, each brother contributing 11s per week. He was a worker and was about to marry the prisoner. What motive was there to kill him? He then turned to Robert Robson Cotton, the prisoner's 14-month-old baby. Kilburn had testified to the child being bounced on his mother's knee, prattling to her. It was repulsive to suggest she would poison him. At this point Mary Ann began to weep as he spoke of her baby. He argued that there was no motive to get rid of the baby, rather there was an instinct to preserve his life. She was the one who had sought medical help for the baby. He reminded the jury that, as a nurse, she would know that medical men would have the skill to find out any wrongdoing. Why then would she invite them in? She had no motive to murder the child and her urgency to get medical help was the act of an innocent mother and not 'by design' as the prosecution had suggested. The prosecution had not produced one atom of evidence of motive in the previous deaths. Again he stressed the point that Nattrass had been supporting the prisoner financially and was to marry her. The evidence produced had shown that the prisoner was kind to the brothers and that they had continued to live in the house for two months after Nattrass's death, and had seen nothing wrong. He asked the jury to consider what actual evidence they had heard about the case under trial before them today, the death of Charles Edward Cotton.

He then turned to the evidence of Isabella Smith. She had worked for twenty-six years at the infirmary and remembered the prisoner being a nurse there on a particular day. The prosecution wanted to imply the prisoner had a scientific knowledge of poisons. But Smith had said this was not so. Nurses only went to the surgery to get medicines already made up. She had said she knew nothing about medicines. If, after twenty-six years, she knew nothing about medicines, how, Foster asked, would the prisoner know anything of them after only eleven months there? He asked the jury to consider why that evidence had been introduced. He argued that it was to put into the minds of the jury that the prisoner had some knowledge of the nature of poisons. Furthermore, he questioned the point of Sarah Smith's evidence. The judge interjected that she had described the symptoms. Foster argued that her evidence was called simply to produce a prejudice in the minds of the jury. He referred to Mary Ann Dodds, who also described the symptoms and the boy being put on the sofa. The prosecution had tried to suggest that putting the boy on the sofa was cruel, but Foster argued that it was, in fact, an act of kindness to wrap the boy up and put him there so as not to be disturbed [by his mother using the bed]. Mary Ann had been unhappy with Chalmers's treatment and had called in Kilburn as well. This, Foster argued, was an act of an innocent, concerned mother.

He then turned to the arsenic soap purchased from Townsend's chemist. He argued that this had been put on the bedstead and rubbed into the walls as testified by Mary Dodds. The green wallpaper had also been a cause of arsenic in the room. He went through a long argument that the amount of arsenic in the soap supplied was all over the bed and walls and could have been ingested by the child. Mary Dodds said there was some left over in a jug, but that jug was never found by the police in their search of Mary Ann's property. He referred to the evidence of the mistreatment of the boy by the Davidsons and that of Priestly. He suggested this was over exaggerated. The amount of insurance money, argued to be a motive, was a measly amount and could not be a real motive. He asked the jury then to consider the making up of the medicines by Chalmers and Kilburn. The likeness of bismuth to arsenic, both white powders, was an issue. He suggested that it was possible for even the most experienced doctor to make a mistake. He argued that the jury had to decide, based on the evidence in this case alone, whether there was any reasonable doubt. He cautioned the jury that, as honest men, they should give an honest verdict, and say that the prisoner was not guilty.

Foster had done his best. He had delivered his services to the prisoner to a high degree. Her fate was now in the hands of the jury. The court then adjourned for twenty minutes.

On his return, Mr Justice Archibald complimented the English Bar, for its readiness to take up the cause of an undefended prisoner at the shortest of notice. He spoke of the serious and grave nature of the charge against the prisoner. He advised the jury to lay aside all they had heard outside the court and only consider the evidence they had heard in the trial. The jury, he said, should start from a presumption of innocence until the prisoner was proved guilty. It had to be proven that there was wilfulness and malice aforethought. Archibald went on to tell the jury that there were certain crimes that could not have direct evidence of the event, such as conspiracy carried on in secrecy. He therefore advised them that the law did not take notice of motive, although it may play a part in evidence, but the prosecution had to show intention. Therefore they had to rely on evidence that would produce a moral certainty of a kind that would be acted on by any reasonable man in the ordinary matters of life, whether direct or indirect. He advised them that direct evidence was not possible in this case. All they could do was seek a certainty that avoided any reasonable doubt. If they arrived at such a moral certainty of guilt, then they had to return a guilty verdict.

He told them that they could not decide the matter on the suggestions of counsel for the prosecution or defence but must decide on the evidence they had heard. That evidence, he said, was in the main circumstantial or indirect evidence. However, circumstantial evidence was the result of the proof by direct evidence of certain facts that were beyond dispute. The judge continued to explore the evidence of Scattergood and of Foster's arguments about the arsenic in the bodies. Even if arsenic had been found in the bodies, then it had to be seen by which mode it got there. Did it get there before or after death? They must then move on to decide if the poison got there by accidental or deliberate means. It is possible that it had been inhaled or ingested by accident through the mouth or breathed in through the lungs. He allowed the possibility that the poison could be taken in through medicine by mistake. He also rehearsed the arguments of counsel that the poisoning could have been through washing. The jury would have to decide this before they moved to consider other things. When they excluded these possibilities, they had to address the question of deliberate administration of the poison and by whom. They had to consider means and opportunity. Whilst they could not rely on direct evidence of the prisoner administering the poison, they had to consider who else might have done so.

They also had to consider the collateral evidence of the other deaths. The prisoner was not on trial for these deaths, only for the death of Charles Edward Cotton. The evidence was only allowed on the question of whether the death of Charles Edward was accidental or not and everything else should be put out of their minds. The judge pointed out that the evidence before the jury in parts could be seen to suggest the innocence of the prisoner, in sending for medical help, or it could be seen as an attempt to disguise wrongdoing. He strongly advised the jury that if there were any suggestions of reasonable doubt that the prisoner administered the poison, they must return a not guilty verdict. On the other hand, if they had a moral certainty that the prisoner and no one else had administered the poison then they must return a guilty verdict. A juryman wanted to ask a question, to the irritability of the judge, as to the quantity bismuth and the quantity of arsenic found in the stomach. Scattergood was called and said he could not remember the quantities. Kilburn was also called to answer and said 15 minims but added that he had no white arsenic powder at his surgery. Surprisingly this was not challenged, as Chalmers had testified that they did. Foster would make a public point of this the next day in the newspaper.

The jury retired to consider their verdict, and a bigamy trial was commenced whilst they deliberated. It was about an hour later that case was interrupted to announce the jury was ready to return. On their return, the Clerk asked the jury:

Do you find the prisoner, Mary Ann Cotton, guilty of the wilful murder of Charles Edward Cotton?

Mary Ann was holding tightly onto the dock rail.
Mr Greener of Darlington, the jury foreman, answered:

Guilty.
As do you all say?
Yes.

The judge donned the traditional black cap and in the usual manner, turning to the prisoner the clerk asked Mary Ann, 'Have you anything to say why sentence of death should not be passed upon you'

Mary Ann replied in a very weak and desperate voice that was almost inaudible, 'I am not guilty'.

It was devastating for Mary Ann. Her response was inaudible and had to be repeated to the judge. She insisted that she was not guilty. The judge's address to Mary Ann was direct and forthright and worth repeating:

Mary Ann Cotton, you have been convicted after a patient and careful trial, of the awful crime of murder. You have had the benefit of the assistance of counsel for your defence, and everything that could be possibly urged on your behalf has been said, but the jury have been led to the only conclusion, to which they could have come, that you are guilty. You have been found guilty of murdering, by means of poison, your step-son, whom you ought to have cherished, and taken care of. You seem to have given way to that most awful of delusions which sometimes takes possession of persons wanting proper moral and religious sense, that you could carry out your wicked designs without being detected, and that you could carry them in secret. But whilst death by poisoning is the most detestable of all crimes, and one at which human nature shudders, it is one which in the order of God's providence, leaves behind it most clear traces of guilt. These warnings, however, come too late, but I feel bound to utter them, that all others who feel tempted to follow your wicked example, may be warned by your miserable fate and punishment. For yourself, in these last words which I shall address to you. I would earnestly urge you to seek for your soul the only refuge that is left for it, in the mercy of God through the atonement of Jesus Christ. It only remains for me to pass upon you the awful sentence of the law which is for you to be taken from hence to the place of execution, and that you be there hanged by the neck until you shall be dead; and that your body be afterwards buried within the precincts of the prison in which you shall have last been confined after your conviction. May the Lord have mercy on your soul.

Mary Ann had been standing throughout the judge's address. Her lips were moving and she trembled violently and as the judge finished, she seemed almost to collapse and need the support of the deputy warden and those close beside her. According to reports, the court, which had been packed solid and silent during the judge's sentencing, broke into 'a profound and chilly murmuring'. Mary Ann was carried from the dock, in a state of insensibility from the shock of verdict and sentencing.

The judge asked Russell if there was any intention of proceeding in the other three cases to which he replied that there was not.

The Durham Goal governor, Charles Armstrong, wrote to the Home Secretary, the official letter required under the court rules, informing him of the verdict and the date of execution, as being Monday, 24 March 1873. This was confirmed to the Home Secretary by Richard Bowser the Under-Secretary for the county.

It became clear that there was no hope of a reprieve and Mary Ann began to accept that death was now inevitable.

There was no shortage of requests to adopt her child. From every station in life there was someone who was prepared to give the child a home. In West Auckland there was a childless couple by the name of Edwards living in Johnson Street, where Mary Ann had lived. Lowrey, the old lodger of Mary Ann's, was writing to her and when the Edwards heard of this, they added a request that they would like to have the child and promised to be good parents for Margaret. It was finally decided that the Edwards would become the child's parents and duly, on 19 March 1873, the Edwards and Lowrey took the train to Durham to collect this precious gift. *The Northern Echo* reported the handing over in detail. Mrs Edwards describes the scene as heavily charged with emotion. She herself was nearly overcome with the strain of it all, and needed her husband and Lowrey to see her through. She reported that Mary Ann did not make any fuss about the releasing of the baby and two hours was spent at the prison. During that time Mary Ann continually stressed that she had not murdered her step-son and frequently proclaimed her innocence. At one point she stated emphatically:

If they put a rope around my neck it will not matter: I never murdered him, I am as innocent as that bairn there [pointing to the baby Margaret]

The scene was truly one of contradiction. Here was a woman charged and found guilty of murder yet here she was, tenderly nursing her child while the flickering light of the fire danced around her, covering them in a warm glow. Her face was as proud as any mother's, her eyes moist from the impending loss of her baby. Mary was wearing a very decent, and for that time, expensive, checked shawl and, when the time came for parting,

Mary Ann handed the child to Mrs Edwards. She removed the shawl from her shoulders and, in a last act of kindness, tore the shawl in two. With the greatest tenderness, she took the child and wrapped her in the shawl, against the cold and damp day that waited outside. She handed the baby back to Mrs Edwards, her eyes filled with tears. Mrs Edwards, also filled with emotion, could wait no longer and turned to leave:

Goodbye, Mrs Cotton

Mary Ann looked at her, and with a sense of great import, said:

Goodbye, and mind the bairn. And mind when you take it home with you to West Auckland, promise me you'll never let Riley come near where she is – and never – no never – and if it should be bad you promise me you'll never have Dr Kilburn for to attend it. Will you Promise?

In the moment and the emotional pressure nothing else but 'yes' would suffice. The Edwards and Lowrey then left Durham prison and caught the train back to West Auckland.

It is a hard heart that is not moved by what was left behind in Durham. Mary Ann was now all alone in terms of family. The baby, when with her, was a symbol of hope of the possibility of reprieve. The baby's leaving brought home to Mary Ann the cold, harsh reality that death by hanging was now the only certain thing she had to look forward to. Margaret Edith Quickmanning had gone, and Mary Ann would never set eyes on her daughter again.

Chapter 11

The Execution

After the trial and conviction there was a surprising outcry suggesting that Mary Ann had had a bad deal. There were many appeals sent to the Home Secretary. The Queen was even asked to intervene. The much respected medical magazine *The Lancet* argued that the eminent Dr Scattergood was wrong in respect of the possibility of arsenic from the air being ingested. The magazine suggested direct evidence against Mary Ann was very slight. Even some of the sensationalist newspapers began to raise questions about the case and the possibility of a commutation of the death sentence to imprisonment. The whole idea of accidental poisoning was also raised. Religious figures along with people from Barnard Castle, Darlington and Bishop Auckland raised petitions calling for mercy. However, all these efforts were to no avail. The Home Secretary refused all appeals and the sentence was confirmed, Mary Ann would hang.

The first relative to visit Mary Ann was Margaret Stott. She was the wife of George Stott's brother. Her visit was a very disheartening one for Mary Ann who protested that her step-father should have visited her by now. Mary Ann encouraged the setting up of petitions supporting her claims of innocence, but Margaret Scott was unhelpful, telling her instead to prepare for her death. She also wrongly told her there was no hope for a reprieve and the two-hour visit ended in terrible agony for Mary Ann, with a lengthy weeping session. The report ended with the statement:

Mrs Stott, who fully believes her to be guilty, says that she is of such an extraordinary temper, and disposition that she will never confess her crimes.

As she continued to await death, Mary Ann was finally visited by her step-father. From the beginning, he had not concerned himself with his step-child. The report of the visit appeared in the newspaper:

On Saturday last, Mr George Stott, deputy-overman of Seaham Colliery, stepfather to the culprit, Mary Ann Cotton, proceeded to Durham Goal for the purpose of visiting her for the first time since her incarceration. Mr Stott encountered little difficulty in gaining admission. After giving up his watch and other things at the entrance door, he proceeded, accompanied by a warder, to the place where Mrs Cotton is confined, which is in the room already described. On entering, there were two female warders in attendance and Mrs Cotton was seated upon a stool beside a good fire. The condemned woman on seeing Mr Stott, immediately jumped up, threw her arms around his neck, and cried, "Oh father, father, I knew you would come and see me." She burst into a fit of crying, and a lengthened time elapsed before one word was exchanged, when she commenced enquiring of some of her relatives. Afterwards Mr Stott informed her that he had delayed visiting her until this time, knowing that if she would confess, she would confess to him. Mr Stott said, "Now, Mary Ann, thou hast not long to live now; and if thou hast anything to confess, do so now." She replied, "Father, I have not led a good life, but I am innocent of the crimes held to my charge. I know the public are against me, but I am going to die for a crime I am as innocent of as the child unborn. I never intentionally gave that boy anything to destroy him. It was in the arrowroot that I bought for him from a grocer in West Auckland when he was ill. I asked for some, and he emptied a drawer. There was not a sufficient quantity to make up the weight, so he pulled out another drawer and teamed something out which was not the colour of the arrowroot, and that is what poisoned him." Mr Stott said, "Why did you not draw attention of the shopkeeper?" She replied that she was confused. Mr Stott said she had one of the best counsellors in England. Why had she not mentioned this important matter to him? She said she entrusted her defence to an attorney, and he advised her to say nothing. He afterwards gave up the case and she had no thoughts of it when placed upon her trial. Mr Stott had some conversation with her with reference to her mother, which he will not divulge. He will not say whether she poisoned her or not, but her wicked habits tended to shorten her mother's days. Mrs Cotton said she had committed bigamy, but what was she to do when that bad man Robinson drove her to the door? Mr Stott, after a lengthy stay, rose to depart. He says he never witnessed such a sight. It was painful to the extreme. He pledged himself that he would, at her request, see Robinson. After leaving he could hear from some considerable distance her cries. Mr Stott says that he has brought her up from being a child, and he knows she would not confess to any person but him; and if guilty, she will die without ever making a confession. He describes her as being neat and clean, with a good dress on and a white collar on her neck, and he never saw her look so well. Other relatives were at the gate asking for permission to enter but were refused.

It would appear that the reporter obtained this information from George Stott. In many ways, it looked like a mission to obtain a confession from Mary Ann. We again hear Mary Ann claim her innocence and, interestingly, allude to a non-intentional poisoning, referring to the arrowroot. The desperate state of Mary Ann is seen in the greeting and farewell. If true, and we must be cautious because George Stott may have been exaggerating his importance, then it would seem reconciliation had happened. The mystery of what was exchanged about the mother is strange. If Mary Ann was innocent of any charge of murdering her mother, would not Stott have made that clear? Speculation was rife at the time and it is a strange step-father who would not clear his child's name. In not doing so, he created a question mark over Mary Ann that remains to this day. Or was George silent because the conversation had involved Mary Ann raising the question of Mrs Paley? There is a reference to other relatives who wanted admission. We do not know who they were.

Before the terrible day of execution there was one other visitor. He was the Rev Stevenson. He regularly visited Mary Ann in her last days. A very decent human being and Christian, he brought great comfort to

Mary Ann. He encouraged her reading of the Bible and Christian books. No doubt he would gently bring Mary Ann to consider all matters concerning the charges and to prepare for that time when she would shortly depart this world.

In her final hours, two things appeared to be of great concern to Mary Ann; her baby, who had been handed over to the Edwards, and the fact that her husband, James Robinson, had not visited her. The newspaper reports speak of periods of weeping in the days before the execution.

The hangman was to be William Calcraft. He was born in Little Barrow in Essex in 1800. At the time of Mary Ann Cotton's execution, he was aged 73 and was approaching the end of his career. Although he had had a 'wife' and children, there was never a record of his having married. Now a widow, his address in the 1871 Census showed him as a 'servant' living at the County Goal in Bedford. His career in the penal system started when he was paid to flog young inmates of Newgate prison for 10s a week. Before embarking on a career as hangman, Calcraft had worked as a shoemaker, a watchman, a butler and a street hawker in London.

He rose to become the City of London's executioner in April 1829 and eventually became England's most well-known hangman. His entry in *The National Biography* describes him as of 'kindly disposition', very fond of his children and grandchildren and loving his pigeons and pets. He died in December 1879,

William Calcraft.

six years after Mary Ann's execution. His arrival in Durham was on the Saturday before the hanging. His assistant would be Robert Evans from Wales.

Robert Evans had changed his name to Robert Anderson (Evans). Born in 1816 and a doctor by qualification, though he never actually practiced medicine. He was a farmer and landowner and could live by private means. It is thought he had a morbid fascination with hanging and in fact paid Calcraft his assistant's fee to work with him. He was, however, a hangman in his own right from 1873 to 1883. He was not an efficient hangman and some of his victims did not die instantly. He was refused the appointment to chief hangman when it became available. He died in 1901, at 85 years of age.

Calcraft had a reputation as a poor hangman, often having to finish the job by pulling on the legs of his victims. In some cases the poor wretch did not die instantly and remained alive for some time – for fifty minutes in the worst case.

On the morning of the execution, Mary Ann was attended by her spiritual advisers and it is claimed she indicated she may have been the agent of the poisonings but they were never wilful, claiming the arrowroot and the use of the arsenic soap in her home. Mary Ann rose very early on the morning of her execution at 3.30 am. At 5.30 she had a cup of tea, but wanted nothing to eat. The scaffold had been prepared and the pit beneath dug out to Calcraft's specifications. A crowd began to gather outside the prison and inside reporters gathered to watch the spectacle. Calcraft did not like the presence of these men and made it plain by asking for them to be locked out.

Out of sight of these reporters in her cell, the ministers attending to Mary Ann had brought calmness to her. She prayed for her wardresses, for James Robinson and her baby. In the privacy of the cell she was pinioned by the executioner with a belt around her chest holding her arms tight against her. At 7.50 am, the sound of the prison bell rang out, telling all present that the execution was proceeding. As the clock began its strike of 8.00 am the procession left the building housing Mary Ann's cell. Accompanied by the prison officials, the Bishop Auckland sheriff's officers, the wardresses, the prison chaplain and Mary Ann's own Wesleyan ministers, especially the Rev Stevenson, Mary Ann walked to the scaffold. Her ministers were praying and Mary Ann was supported either side by a male warder. She walked erect and her face was observed as being 'with deep emotion'. She was apparently praying and as she exited the building she was heard to say, 'heaven is my home'. She was dressed in black with her head and neck uncovered. The other half of the black and white shawl that she had shared with her baby covered her shoulders. It covered the leather straps that held her arms. She never diverted her attention from prayers and the utterance, 'Lord have mercy', was heard. Eventually she stood on the scaffold and Calcraft covered her head and face with a white cap. By now Mary Ann was trembling visibly and in continual prayer. Robert Evans placed the noose around Mary Ann's neck. Calcraft then strapped her legs together. Calcraft moved to make a final adjustment of the rope. Mary Ann was seen to clasp her hands tightly. She again exclaimed, 'Lord have mercy on my soul'. At the arranged signal, Robert Evans drew the bolt. Mary Ann dropped into the void beneath, her neck dropping to one side. Her body jerked heavily and Calcraft put his hands on her shoulders. On releasing his hands, Mary Ann's body continued to jerk. Reports said it took three minutes for the body to subside from its twitching. Bowser, the under-sheriff, was overcome and fainted, being caught by the two male warders before he fell. Upon her death, the black flag was raised over the prison in the usual manner, indicating to the crowd outside that the execution had been carried out.

The body of Mary Ann was laid in a black coffin. The identification of the body was made by Margaret Robinson, aged 49, the matron at Durham Goal, along with Mary Hannah Nellis a sub-matron, aged 30, who had looked after Mary Ann and the baby. An inquest was held in the prison schoolroom, and it confirmed the death by hanging, which would appear on the death certificate. There was an argument about the rope not being in the coffin with the body, and despite an objection by a jury man, it was ruled that there was no law which demanded the rope be in the coffin. A surprising visitor to the inquest, accompanied by a friend, was Margaret Stott, who was so sure Mary Ann was guilty. It is said that she sobbed horrendously and had to be supported by her companion. Mary Ann was buried in the prison grounds, beside two others who had been hung in 1869. Mary Ann Cotton's life was over and in reflecting what the Bard had written many years ago, '…the good of Mary Ann Cotton was interred with her bones, and the evil she was claimed to have done lives on after her.'

Chapter 12

Mary Ann Cotton's Prison Letters

On 7 March 1873, after her trial, Mary returned to Durham Gaol. Her execution was scheduled for 8.00 am on 24 March 1873. She was obviously shaken by the sentence and wrote a number of letters from her cell. On 10 March 1873, the following letter was sent to a Bishop Auckland businessman, George Moore, who lived in Tenters Street with his wife, Elizabeth, and their six children. The letters are presented here as she wrote them.

Durham County Jail 10th March 1873

Sir, I will take it as a great favour if you will call and see me at your convenience. Will you please to ask Mr Labron to come with you. I wish to consult with you about getting a petition for my life to be spared. You must get a Visiting Justice order to come in, and must tell him what your business is with me. Mr Fawcett Smith Bailey, Durham, is one, and Mr J F Elliot, Elvet Hill, Durham is another. Either of them will give you an order for me.

yours respectfully   M A COTTON

At the time, the newspapers assumed Mary Ann had written it herself, and claimed it proved she was better educated than she pretended. However, when compared to other letters, it is more likely this was written for her by a warder or other gaol officer. The grammar, punctuation and spelling are all superior to other letters she was known to have written. The letter was written on the Monday morning after her sentence and appears to be her first considered reaction. The letter does not say

155

anything about her guilt as she appears to want to make her cause out him face to face. Unfortunately, he was unable to help her in this matter.

In the letter Mary Ann displays her bitterness at Thomas Riley and complains how her legal representative had let her down. Her insistence of her innocence is expressed strongly and she would maintain this until her death.

She also wrote to her husband, James Robinson (they had never divorced).

March the 12
my dear frends
I so pose you Will mor than I can tell you con serning my Afull faite I have come I wish to know if you will Let me see the 3 childer as soune as you possible you can I should Like to see you Bring them if you can not Aske sum Won Eals to Bring them I have been told to day you say you onley had Won Letter from me since I left you if you have not got Enny mor they have been detaineg from you ie hope you Will get this And I thinke if you have Won sarke of kindness in you Will Try to get my Life spared you know your sealfe there has been A moast dredfull to hear tell of the Lyes that have been told A Bout me ie must tell you Art h Cause of All my trouble fore if you had not Left the house And So As I coud hav got in to my house When I came the dor i Was to Wandr the streets With my Baby in my Armes no home fore me no plase to Lay my head you Know if you call your mind Backe I shoud not solde my things in susicke street to come to you then I had mother to call on then But When you closed the dore I had no Won for you Know your sealfe I am Knot guilty of the Lyies that has been tolde Consirning me if you spoake the nothing But the trouth I can not draw my mind on the past for it is mor than natur can bare Won thing I hope you Will try to get my Life spared for ie Am not guilty of the crime ie have to dyie fore consider things And do What you Can fore me so ie must Conclude A this time I hope to hear from you By return of post.

you K W…….
M A R   M A Cotton

This letter has been referred to previously, but what we can add here is that Mary Ann's request to see the '3 childer' is either a cynical ploy for ammunition to get a reprieve or a genuine desire to see the children she had cared for. It is notable that she wishes to see all three surviving Robinson children, not just her own son, George. Again she insists on her innocence and also refers to previous correspondence that she had written to James. Her claim that the letters were 'detaineg from you' was probably a swipe at James's sisters, with whom Mary Ann never got on. She blames them for James not receiving her letters. Despite all that has happened between Mary Ann and James, in her desperation she appeals to her former lover and husband to help her.

Another letter was written to one Henry Holdforth, which was referred to earlier.

My der frend
I reseved your most Kind and Welcome Letter this morning whitch it hirt my feelings very much you say you have read my case in the papers Well my der frend I hope you Will not Juge me rong as I have been on the ampill crime of murder of Charles Edward Cotton I am not guilty of it thoe to reade the evedens that comes in aganst me you may think I am but if ie must Tell you I am not guilty. Evidens Was never given propley in to the Counsler or I should not come to what I have for I had a first class Counsler to defend me but I should like if I could get A portison up to spare my Life. You speak of mother, had I my mother I should not been hear, fore my father I have seen him since mother Death, that is 6 years 15th of this month, so he has no mor feeling now than he had When We had mother, but thanke god she is hope in heaven, she Left evry resons to beleaiv she Was happy, mt dearly bloved Brother, father, Robson, and my husbent W Mawbray, and my Dear Childe is there so I shall hope to meet them on the othe side of Jonion the time you speak of my dark eyes I Was happy then, and them Was days of Joy to all of our soles, but this Last 6 years my Life has been miserable sore I marriet a Man they call James Robinson, he had 3 sisters I never Was Looked on as I should be With nor of them. He said I could not Ergree We had sum Words a boute sum money and

I Left the house for a few days, I did not Wish to part from him As I had no home I went to south hetton, stayed ther When I returned their was na home fore me he had sold What he did not Want And tooke the othe things and Went to Live With his sister so I mite go Where I Liked so I got mariet to this Man Cotton he dide the Month Afte We come to Auckland to tell you All the past, I can not as it is to hartrenden to think on I should Like if you could Write to gorge hall And do What you can fore me to be spared With my Life, I have no frends to Looke After me, nothing But strangers What has only knone me A few months, so I hope And trust in god you Will do All you Can And get gorge hall to do the same I do not know what to write to him so I must Come to a Close give my kind love to All that know me hoping they Will do the same do for Well I must say thar Will not be enny mor Sunday schoule for me now, but I shall try to put my trust in god As you know I Wens did And there was non on earth happier than I was then but He says he Will not leave us in trouble, I will nor Leave th all mine enemys whisper together against me, even against me do they imagine this evil, So no mor from A friendless Woman ho I may say is forsaken By the World, but I hope not by god
M A COTTON
Write Wonse mor to me Let my case be known to all that know Me I hope meet All my frends in heaven

She stresses that she is not guilty of the crimes: not the one she was convicted of nor all the other accusations. There is some regret at ever marrying James Robinson, but when he closed the door, she was left alone. Obviously George Stott was not considered as someone she could go back to after she had taken things from the house and the row that ensued. Is there also a woman in these letters who may be realising her folly? She recalls the happier time of marriage to Mowbray and the earlier days at the Methodist church – '…and them Was days of Joy to all our soles….' There is also evidence of a Christian background when referring to Scripture and taking comfort in her faith. Holdforth's daughter, Elizabeth (born in South Hetton), and his son, William, were probably friends of Mary Ann in her youth at the Methodist chapel. In desperation, she was calling in anyone she could think of to help her. She also refers to George Hall as one of those who should be recruited to help in her desire for a petition. George Hall was born in Haswell, close to South Hetton. It is likely he was a teenage love interest of Mary Ann. He worked as a miner at Shotton Colliery at the time of Mary Ann's trial. It would be very strange if he was unaware of the events concerning Mary Ann. The newspapers throughout the region had been full of all the details, including her past. Yet he had not made any attempt to contact her. Indeed, she ends the letter with the realisation that her earthly chances are poor and her only hope now was God. If we can lay aside any prejudice, we can ask if this letter is one of an innocent woman or that of a scheming murderess.

James Robinson did not reply to the first letter and, as we saw earlier, Mary Ann wrote again. She was desperate and again she appeals to James, asking him this time to meet up with her aunt at Monkwearmouth, Sunderland. He did not do as she asked and in fact never saw her again. He turned up at the prison with his brother in law, who went into see Mary Ann. He was of no help and only urged Mary Ann to confess. She maintained her innocence as she does here in this letter:

My der frend
As I Can not say Enny thing Ealse to you my Last request is to you Will you meeat Ant Hulbard tomorrow After now forn 3 to 4 in the Afternoone you Will meeat hir beside the Banke yon side of the Bridge MunkWormouth she Wans to see you ie Wrote to try to get A portivhion to get my Life spared And to come out And Stand the tryill for the other 3 cases thot I ame carged With for ie Am not guilty of them my proper Evidens Was not propley given to the Counsleur ie should not have been condemd to death I ingaeged A man they Call him Smith I thate he Was a solisete At frist Whun he come to me he got A bout £20 bloing to me for my first case he tolde me on the day I Was tryied At Auckland ie Was not t Speake A Single Worde And that mr Blackwell and greenhow Would be thare to defende mee When ie Went in to the docks thore Was nowon for me the Jugdge A pointed the Counsler ie must say he was A clever man to for if he had My propr defence I should Won

th tryile so I hope you Will meat hir ny Last requet
Farewell from M A R or M A Cotton

It is also to be noted that she would have wanted to be tried on the other three charges as well - such was her confidence that with a better defence she would not be found guilty.

Two more letters were printed in the press, written by Mary Ann just before she was executed. One was a statement sent to Lowrey:

March th 22 1873
My der frend,
I did not give Mistr Smith Authority to get the pawn tickets from mary Ann Dodds, I did not know he had got them till Hurchinson At Bishop Auckland told me.
MARY ANN COTTON
Witness, Mary Douglass
Schoolmistress, County Goal, Durham

The second was a response to letters from the Mr and Mrs Edwards, who had taken her daughter, and Mr Lowrey.

My dear friends
I received yours this morning And happy to hear my Baby Was Well I hope by the healpe of god she Will grow in grase And repay you for your kindness to her I hope she Will be A Blessing to you both so you must Excuse my short note to you As ie feale unable to Write more hoping We Will All Meeat in heaven At gods Write hand Where ther Will be no mor pain
Yours affnelnedly
MARY ANN COTTON
March th 22, 1873   Kiss my babe for me

Only the hardest heart could read this last letter and not be moved. This is a woman who is on the brink of death, and is overcome with emotion cannot write anymore. Her last written word, as far as we know, was to send a kiss to her child.

MARY ANN COTTON'S PRISON LETTERS

On 19 March 1873, a letter from Lowrey appeared in *The Northern Echo*.

Sir, I am a constant reader of your valuable paper. Perhaps you will be kind enough to grant me a small space in it and I will tell you what my friends and I have seen in prison to-day. I got a letter from Mrs. Cotton last week, asking me to try and get up a petition to save her life. I sent her word back that I thought there would be no chance for her, and told her in my simple way to come to the cross of Christ, for he says "Let your sins be as red as scarlet, I will make them as white as snow." "Be that cometh unto me I will in no wise cast out."

When I was writing to her, Mr. and Mrs. Edwards told me to ask her if she would give them her baby, and they would assure her that they would bring it up in the fear of God. I got a letter last night. It came by train, and the St. Helens station-master brought it down. Many thanks for his kindness. She said her days were getting short on this earth. She was quite willing for Mr. Edwards to have the baby, and very thankful to him besides for his kindness. So we were up by the lark this morning, and arrived at the prison about 9.30 a.m. We had a little bit of trouble in getting it; but thanks to Mr. Fawcett, be gave us an order for admission. So, after leaving our watches and little property at the office inside the door, we were taken to the cell where the unhappy woman was. I found the cell fifty times better than I expected. Everything was as clean as a new pin. The first thing I saw was Mrs. Cotton sitting on a stool close by a good fire, giving the breast to her infant. She was dressed in a skirt, a loose jacket, but no shoes on, and nothing on her head. Looking round the cell I saw three chairs, one table, a bed, and some rood books. The table had pretty paper on. There was one window on the south side, and the sun was shining on it. In fact, she seems to have every comfort that this earth can afford. God forbid, Mr. Editor, that I should ever see such sight again. Just imagine a little child on its mother's knee, looking up in its mother's face and laughing, and her on the brink of another world. ml her heart as hard as atone. I talked to her a

161

good bit about another world. These are the words she said "I wish I may never have power to rise off this seat. I never give that boy, C.E. Cotton, any poison wilfully." She said, "It was the arrowroot, and we all got It. I am going to die for a crime I am not guilty of. But. nevertheless, we got the child home all right. It has a kind father and mother. May God bless them. I may just any the female warders are very kind her.— I am, Sir, your obedient servant, W. Lowrey. West Auckland, March 19, 1873.

She is reported once more to have given a very powerful assertion of innocence and refers to arrowroot she believed was contaminated with poison. This was arrowroot she had bought from Thomas Riley's shop. It was part of the substances taken by the police for analysis. But no analysis of the arrowroot was produced in evidence. The homely picture of Mary Ann and her baby is again a poignant one. Soon she would be separated from her child and the assertions of innocence ignored.

Chapter 13

The Aftermath

The Reverend Montford, who had spoken with Mary Ann before her execution, raised a stir when he claimed that Mary Ann had made a confession to him. It transpired that all she had said was that she 'may' have been the agent of the poisoning but it was 'unintentional', which is what she always claimed because of the arrowroot mix-up and cleaning soap. Following Mary Ann's execution, stories began to emerge about her time in prison. One such report was that a piece of soap that had gone missing which, after a search, was found hidden up Mary Ann's sleeve. People accused her of wanting to use it to harm her baby. This is certainly untrue as Mary Ann was reported by her warders as always loving and caring towards her daughter. However, it is more likely that Mary Ann may have intended to use it for herself to make her ill and delay the execution.

After Mary Ann's death two men from Hartlepool were allowed to take a cast of Mary Ann's head. To achieve this, her hair had to be cut off. On completion, James Young, the prison's deputy governor, made sure that every single strand of the hair was replaced in the coffin with Mary Ann's body.

This photograph of Mary Ann was first put on sale by a photographer in Durham. On 12 April, at The West Auckland Fair, a group of wax works were displayed and the one that drew the most visitors was the effigy of Mary Ann Cotton in the

Mary Ann Cotton photographed at the time of her trial.

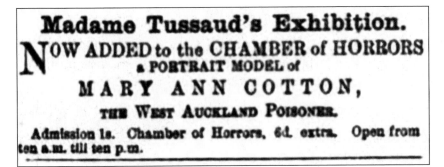

Madame Tussaud's advertisement after Mary Ann's conviction.

condemned cell, and was on view in the middle of the village green, just opposite Mary Ann's old house. By June of that year, Madame Tussaud's was also exhibiting a model of Mary Ann in the Chamber of Horrors.

On 12 April 1873 the *Figaro* newspaper in London reviewed the play, *The Life and Death of Mary Ann Cotton*, which was performed at the West Hartlepool Theatre of Varieties. It commented: 'A delicious horror was offered the other day to the morbid population of West Hartlepool'. The actress Miss E. Leighton was said to be the very image of Mary Ann. The editor of *The Northern Echo* was indignant and asked 'what the magistrates or Licencing Authorities of West Hartlepool were about'. The play, he said, was 'disgusting' and expressed surprise that any actress would play 'the poor wretch' who had paid for her crimes.

A report appeared in the *Nottinghamshire Guardian* on 11 April 1873, explaining what had happened to the rope used to hang Mary Ann. Apparently, Calcraft had secured if for his assistant Robert Evans, whose hobby was collecting the nooses of hangings he had attended. The report claimed that he had these nooses hanging up all around his living room.

Another strange event was that, in West Auckland, apparitions of Mary Ann's victims were said to have been seen.

The report in *The Northern Echo* is worth reading to bring a little ray of humour into this dark episode:

A pitman named Thomas Barker, living at Newrow, about half a mile from St Helen's Colliery, had been at a card party at St Helen's and was going home a little after midnight. After passing

THE POLICE NEWS

LAW COURTS AND WEEKLY RECORD

SATURDAY, APRIL 5, 1873.

PRICE ONE PENNY.

STRANGE SPECTRE APPEARANCES OF THE POISONED VICTIMS OF MARY ANN COTTON-AUCKLAND

Police News report on ghosts at St Helen Auckland.

the pit, he states that he saw what he thought was a child, standing by the side of the road. He saluted it, "Ho," but as it gave him no answer, he felt a sinking sensation, and endeavoured to go past, but the spectre, as he now supposed it to be, moved as quick as himself, and kept alongside of him. "Geordy's" terror increased, and he felt his hair gradually rise, until, as he ran, finding the ghost still kept on equal terms with him, his hair stood on his head. When he got to the house he was completely exhausted and almost burst the door open to get in before the spectre and shut it out.; but not so, it was in the house as soon as him, and went direct upstairs. Barker, fortunately, has a wife, having been married two years and she partly pacified him. He would not however, sleep upstairs, but consented to sleep in a cheffionier bed in the downstairs room. They had not, however, been in bed many minutes when he heard the source of his terror walking about the chamber floor making a similar noise to a cat with cockle shells on its feet, and at length they heard a whiz resembling a flight of pigeons, go through the roof, and this was immediately followed by three awful crashes of thunder. Barker and his wife simultaneously leaped out of bed, leaving their young child, and ran out, naked, to the house of a neighbour named Hodgson, some distance along the row. Hodgson's family were soon aroused, and gave them shelter. On hearing their "tale of terror" Hodgson sent his son, at Barker's request, to bring the child out of bed and shut the door, which, in their hurry, they had left open The lad went, but on looking in, soon took to his heels, asserting he had seen the ghost coming down the stairs. Ultimately Hodgson and his wife went and brought the child away, and Barker, who had to go to the pit foreshift, sent to his "marrow" to take his place: and he has since been so terrified that he had no less than eleven comrades at his house on the following night to sit up with them.

Chapter 14

Those Who Were Part of Mary Ann's Story and Outlived Her

George Stott

As we saw earlier, in 1871 George Stott was living at Seaham with his wife, Hannah, and step-son, George Paley. George Stott was absent from Mary Ann's final hours and did not attend at her funeral and burial. It would appear from reports at the time of the trial that he believed Mary Ann to be guilty. As we have already seen, his sister-in-law did attend, and was extremely distressed by the experience. By 1891, George and his family had moved to St Mary Street East in Tunstall, Sunderland, where George was still working as a miner. By 1891 he had retired and went to live with his step-family in Crossley Terrace, in Gateshead. George Stott died in June 1895.

The Potters

Edward and Margaret Potter were kind enough to offer the teenage Mary Ann a position of trust in looking after their children. Edward Potter died on 9 September 1869 at Tynemouth, when Mary Ann was living with James Robinson. Potter's wife, Margaret, inherited his estate, around about £40,000, at historic RPI rates this would be £3 million (2016). She shared the money with her children. Margaret was very complimentary about Mary Ann at the time of her trial, and went on to live in reasonable comfort, dying on 23 June 1876. Her estate of £10,000, (£725,000 today), was left to her children.

James Robinson

Mary Ann's husband went to live at 5 Roseanna Street, Sunderland, with William and Mary Jane, his two children born to Hannah, his wife who

167

DEATH OF THE HUSBAND OF MARY ANN COTTON.

The remains of James Robson, one of the oldest foreman shipwrights on the Wear, were buried on Saturday at Bishopwearmouth Cemetery. Deceased, who was much respected, worked for Messrs Short Bros. for many years, and had retired on a pension allowed by the firm. A large number of shipwrights and other friends followed. The second wife of the deceased was the notorious Mary Ann Cotton, who was hanged at Durham some years ago.

James Robinson's death report in newspaper.

had died before he married Mary Ann. He also had young George, born to Mary Ann and abandoned by her when she had left him. The family also had a new housekeeper, one Frances Pratt from Deptford. In 1873, James married Mary Elizabeth Dixon and moved to 14 Roseanna Street, where we find him in 1881, and the census shows a girl, Alice Robinson, with the description daughter. James died on 4 January 1899, leaving his wife £553/10s, (about £48,000 in today's money). His death did not go un-noticed and a short news item appeared in the press, in which they got his name wrong.

George Robinson

When James Robinson found his young son, George, had been taken by Mary Ann, there is no doubt he would have feared the worst and may have thought he would never see him again. The joy when he was returned to his father on New Year's Day must have been one of great satisfaction. The young lad would grow in strength and follow in his father's trade, becoming a shipwright at the same yard. In June 1889 he married a Sunderland girl, Mary Ann, and settled at Mount Pleasant in Bishopwearmouth, Sunderland. George and Mary Ann were very productive and, by 1911, they were living at 29 Dene Street, Pallion, Sunderland, with their eight children, three boys and five girls. By then, his son, George Henry, had also followed his father into the shipwright trade. One daughter became a baker and another had gone into service.

From such a difficult start in life, George Robinson had forged ahead and there is no doubt his father, James, would have been very proud of him.

Thomas Riley

Mary Ann's nemesis, Thomas Riley, was the son of a miner and in his earliest work life endured the ruggedness of that industry. His toughness, tenacity and forceful character were probably forged in the pits around West Auckland. He worked hard to build up a very decent business in the village and eventually would own property, both in the village and at the nearby Witton Park. He returned to his usual life in West Auckland and

DEATH OF A SOUTH DURHAM WORTHY.
THE UNRAVELLING OF THE COTTON MYSTERY.

Thomas Riley's newspaper death report.

The death is announced of Mr Thomas Riley, of West Auckland, at the age of 76. The deceased was a man of remarkable gifts, and with a grit that earned for him a well-deserved success. He was the son of a miner, and at a very early age had to suffer the hardships of pitlife, from which he freed himself, and founded a successful business for himself. Until recent years deceased had been in the forefront of elections as a Liberal since the time of Lord Harry Vane. The late Mr Riley was a leading supporter of Sir Joseph Pease in all his political struggles in the old South Durham days. The deceased gentleman was an active supporter of the temperance cause, and was a constant attendant at the United Methodist Free Church. He was a considerable owner of property in his native village, and also in Witton Park, South Church, etc. Deceased was historically associated with the case of Mary Ann Cotton, the notorious poisoner; and it was to his courage that this criminal's career was first brought to public investigation. Mr Riley knew Cotton—as, indeed, at that time, he knew perhaps everybody in the village and neighbourhood. He was on the juries which investigated the causes of the deaths in the Cotton family. No one had suspected or hinted the hideous cause of the series of deaths of those whose last moments had been spent in the daring prisoner's society. The late Mr Riley, full of suspicion, approacehd the doctors (since dead) and the police. Mr Riley was in vain warned of the seriousness of the suggestions or accusations he was making, but he persisted, and the result was the sentence and execution of the poisoner.

remained a person of note, always being the man who pursued Mary Ann Cotton to justice. In 1881 we find him living with his wife, Margaret, and one daughter, Margaret Agnes. He was still running a business, this time as a seed merchant. By 1891 we find Thomas Riley has taken up residence in Brookfield Cottage, the house reputedly lived in by the excise man who had been linked to Mary Ann Cotton. The current owners kindly allowed me to visit and let me see the original deeds that Thomas Riley had signed. The house purchase cost £280 on 5 May 1879. He lived there with his wife, Margaret, the same daughter, Margaret Agnes, and a granddaughter who was in residence at the time of the census. He appears, at age 69, to have given up trading and collects tax and rates for the Inland Revenue. His celebrity status had not diminished and a local poet from Bishop Auckland, Bobby Gibbons, dedicated his 1897 collection of Poems, *Visions Past and Present*, to Thomas Riley for his work in catching Mary Ann Cotton. Thomas Riley died the following year on 23 July 1898. In his will he left an estate valued at £1,560, (£136,000 in today's money). A newspaper report on his death lauded his many achievements as a citizen of West Auckland, and recorded his membership of both the temperance movement and the United Methodist Free Church. The greatest plaudit in the report was that he was the one who had persisted, in the face of many who had tried to dissuade him, in his pursuit of the doctors and the police until he got what he believed was justice for the Cottons.

William Byers Kilburn

At the time of Mary Ann's trial, Dr William Byers Kilburn lived on Front Street with his wife, Mary, and their four sons and one daughter. He was born in West Auckland in 1832 and was registered as a surgeon in June 1859. Kilburn was buried at St Helen's Auckland Parish church on 30 October 1886 aged 54 years.

At the west end of the nave of the church, a memorial window was created in his memory.

He died leaving his estate of £280/5s (about £25,000 today) to his widow, Mary.

Dr Byers Kilburn's memorial window at St Helen Auckland church.

Close up of inscription on memorial window.

Sergeant Tom Hutchinson

Sergeant Hutchinson, who was very prominent in the Mary Ann Cotton case, was born in 1838 at Washton, near Richmond in North Yorkshire. He served in Whitby, Jarrow and Whitburn. He moved to Thorne near Doncaster and, whilst there, made a name for himself and was promoted to Police Constable first class. He moved to Wolsingham and was quickly promoted to Sergeant. His move to West Auckland was the one that projected him into the public eye in 1872 as the 'arrester of the infamous West Auckland poisoner'. The year after Mary Ann's execution he was rewarded for his work with promotion to Inspector. He then moved on to Lancaster

Sergeant Tom Hutchinson.

where he was taken seriously ill with typhoid fever. He never fully recovered from the illness and moved first to West Hartlepool and then onto Stockton. He retired in July 1890 with a reputation as an excellent policeman. He settled with his wife, Lucy, and their four daughters in Stokesley, about 30 miles from West Auckland, the scene of his most famous arrest. He died on 20 April 1900, leaving an estate of £582/17s/2d (£49,000 in today's money).

The Excise Man

The question of the excise man at West Auckland is intriguing. Every article and book calls him John Quickmanning, or other variants. Mary Ann even named her child Margaret Edith Quickmanning Cotton. The sworn depositions all state his name as 'Mr Mann the excise officer'. I have searched the birth, death and marriage records, as well as census material for England, Scotland and Wales and have found no evidence that an excise man named Quickmanning existed. A search of the 1871 Census for West Auckland in that year shows no Quickmanning, Mann or any variant living in West Auckland. A search of the Custom and Excise files at The National Archives and West Auckland Brewery records from the time also turned up no one with that name.

The 1861 Census shows a Richard Quick Mann, aged 17 years, living in St Ives and working as a pupil teacher in an elementary school. The 1871 Census throws up a Richard Quick Mann, aged 27 and a revenues officer, boarding in St Ives, Cornwall. This must be the same person. He is described as 'a ride officer'. This is an officer who specialised in inspection of breweries. I am relatively certain that Richard Quick Mann is the revenue officer who was in West Auckland in 1872 to inspect the West Auckland Brewery. The question then arises as to whether he was the father of Mary Ann's child. There is every possibility that Mary Ann may have had her eye on such a man. At 29 years old he would have been ten years younger than Mary Ann and certainly a better catch materially than Joseph Nattrass to whom she was engaged. However, by this time Mary Ann had given birth to at least twelve children and was past her best years. There is no concrete evidence that she ever had a relationship with the excise man. There were just rumours that Mary Ann was happy to allow and would never confirm or deny. Mary Ann Dodds, a neighbour, cleaner and friend of Mary Ann, swore that she did not believe the rumours. The timing of the birth of the baby in 1873 does allow for the possibility that the father was Joseph Nattrass. He was named as such in the local newspaper, the *Morpeth Herald*. So why would Mary Ann give the child a name, part of which was 'Quickmanning'? Mary Ann was not stupid. She had demonstrated her craftiness and ability to work the odds. Giving the baby a name that would suggest a father who had the means to provide a good future for her was a wise and sensible thing, especially in the day when paternity would be hard to confirm or deny. Certainly any name referring to a dead man would not be smart.

Mary Ann was desperate to get help from any source, even an old boyfriend from her youth. If the excise man had been her lover, father of her baby, and a government officer to boot, would not the worldly wise Mary Ann at least attempt to get his help? She writes several letters seeking help, yet not a single one to the excise officer. The fact that she does not do this suggests that there may, in fact, have been no close relationship. There is absolutely no mention of him by Mary Ann in any part of the trial or afterwards, except in reported statements from witnesses. Furthermore, if the baby had been the excise man's, would he not have contacted Mary Ann when he knew she was pregnant and delivered a baby? I am, therefore, reluctant to accept that the excise man

Richard Quick Mann, if indeed it was he who was in West Auckland, was the father of Mary Ann's baby.

Richard Quick Mann was next found in Linton in 1875 when, in September of that year, he married Elizabeth Reeve. He probably worked in the large East Anglian Brewery in that area. Six years after marrying he had already fathered five children. He later moved to Wrexham in North Wales where he settled. It was there he died on 22 March 1912, aged 68. He left an estate to his wife, Elizabeth, of £229/18s, (£23,000 in 2016).

Margaret Edith Quickmanning Cotton

William Edwards, a miner, was born in Evenwood, a few miles from West Auckland. His wife was Sarah Robinson, who was born at St Helen's Auckland. They were married in September 1867, and the union had produced no children. By 1881 they had moved from West Auckland to the nearby village of Merrington.

Margaret Edith Quickmanning Cotton was now formally adopted by the Edwards, and they began to call her Margaret Edwards. By 1891 they had moved to the village of Tudhoe Grange, where they had bought a public house called 'The Garden House'. William was both the barman and a miner at the nearby colliery.

Margaret was not with them at Tudhoe, she had married Joseph Fletcher, a miner, in December 1890. They initially settled at Merrington village.

However in 1873 the Fletcher family, Joseph, Margaret and the first born daughter, Clara, headed to Liverpool and there they boarded *The Umbria* and on 8 May 1873, they landed at Ellis Island in New York. The family made their way to Boston, where Joseph took employment in the mining industry. Margaret became pregnant and a son, William, was born. Life in America was not the greener pasture they had supposed and they

Umbria manifest showing the Fletchers sailing to New York.

struggled to develop a life. Margaret became pregnant again and then disaster struck. Joseph was killed while trying to cross the railway track close to where he was working. Margaret, with two children and pregnant with her third, was devastated. She had only one thought; to get back to the comfort of family in Durham. On 23 October 1894, Margaret, Clara and the baby William, set sail on the *Cephalonia*, which brought them home to Liverpool.

They made their way to 'The Greyhound Inn' at Ferryhill, where Sarah Edwards was running the pub, after the death of William. John Joe was born in 1895. In June 1901, a long time after Joseph's death, Margaret met and fell in love with a Ferryhill man, Robinson Kell, who worked as a hewer at the local mine. In 1902 their first child, Robinson, was born. Margaret began to suffer with increasing eye problems and eventually lost her sight. Margaret had moved a long way from the events surrounding Mary Ann Cotton and had made a good life for herself. Yes,

War graves in France © goforchris' photosteam http://blethers.blogspot.co.uk.

she saw tragedy but she overcame it, as her adventure to America had proven. The negativity and stigma surrounding her origins were contested by the two Fletcher sons. When war broke out William, who had been born in America, joined the Durham Light Infantry and was wounded in action. When recovered he soon transferred to the Rifle Brigade (The Prince Consort's Own) and went to fight in France and Flanders. He was killed in action on 4 November 1918. His army record states 'Died of wounds'.

His brother, John Joe, also joined up with the Alexandra, Princess of Wales's Own (Yorkshire Regiment) 9th Battalion and became a lance corporal. He also served in France and was killed in action. These two grandchildren of Mary Ann Cotton, who had been convicted of taking life, gave their own lives for their country and were a credit to their mother, Margaret.

Margaret continued to live in Ferryhill and died on 19 August 1954. From what is said of her, she was a marvellous woman who, despite an inauspicious start in life, great trials with blindness and the loss of a young husband and two great sons, triumphed over it all; a suitable ending for the story of Mary Ann Cotton.

Chapter 15

Was Mary Ann Cotton the West Auckland Borgia?

In researching Mary Ann Cotton, I have moved from thinking of her as the mass murderer of local legend to a very misunderstood character who may not be guilty of as many deaths, as have been alleged, if any. It has to be acknowledged that if Mary Ann were tried today using the evidence presented in court, the improper chain of evidence, the inconsistency of witnesses and the antics of her defence team at the committal hearings, the outcome would be so different. No one actually testified to seeing Mary Ann administer any arsenic to any person. The argument that she was the only one attending the deceased was contradicted by the Taylor brothers who said Mary Ann had brought a woman in to cook for them. Every single piece of evidence was circumstantial. Even the judge agreed with that. Medical witnesses contradicted each other in the matter of arsenic at the doctor's surgery, where a mistake could have been made. Then there is the difference in opinion on Nattrass's death between Richardson and Scattergood. Does that mean she is an innocent victim? That, I believe, is a very difficult question. What is innocent? If you are alleged to have killed one person or twenty, does it reduce wickedness?

To establish when and if Mary Ann became a murderess is fraught with difficulty. The times she lived in were times when death from illness was extremely common.

I would argue she did not murder the Mowbrays, with the exception of Isabella, where there may be a reasonable doubt. She certainly seemed to have a genuine affection for her husband, William, and we have to keep in mind that doctors had been involved and that all had certified the deaths as natural.

With regards to her mother, this too is doubtful. Margaret Stott did have a serious liver disease and death was certain from it. As noted above, we do not know the stage of the illness or how long Margaret Stott had been ill. From all reports, Mary Ann did seem to have a genuine affection for her mother. The question remains, was the death natural and simply took its course whilst Mary Ann was there, or did someone speed it up? I still maintain that there are questions as to why George Stott would not discuss the issues raised after his visit to Mary Ann in prison. His refusal to answer the question of Mary Ann's guilt is puzzling. Was there a question to be asked about his relationship with the next door neighbour?

It is very unlikely, but not impossible, that any of the Robinson children died at Mary's hands. It was hindsight that brought the accusations. Mary Ann Cotton had discussed with James Robinson the rumours that she was killing the Robinson children and he believed that they were wrong, telling her not to worry about them. He did change his mind at the time of the trial, but was this the response of a wounded husband? Again, doctors had been involved and we know of one other outsider, Mrs Hindmarch, who was present at the death of Isabella Mowbray and the Robinson children. The usual problem arises in the context of the time when, as previously stated, a fever could come into the home and wipe out a whole family. Can we really convict when there is a doubt?

With George Ward, we again see a man who had bad medical advice and who was very ill. His illness was the subject of great scrutiny by three doctors. It has to be noted that it was Mary Ann who called in the second medical opinion for her husband. If she was poisoning him why would she do that? We also know that his illness was a public matter in the town. Would she risk poisoning under all this scrutiny? Whilst we can all speculate, we have to rest on the knowledge that there is no evidence of any kind to confirm Mary Ann murdered him.

There is also no substantial evidence that Mary Ann had a hand in the death of Margaret Cotton. We have to resist looking at her death in the light of Mary Ann's trial and try to reason on available evidence. Those who accused her in Walbottle were certainly not her friends. No evidence exists of her guilt in this matter. Furthermore, the *Police Gazette* on 19 October 1872 carried the following:

It has been definitely ascertained that the woman Mary Ann Cotton had nothing to do with the death of her husband's [Fred Cotton] first wife, or the children of Cotton's sister, which happened at Walbottle, near Newcastle-on-Tyne. The explanation is said to be very clear and satisfactory. The last one, the sister, died in March 1869, and it was not until the 7th of July that the woman who called herself Mary Ann Mowbray came to the village…

In relation to Fred Cotton, Mary Ann certainly did not have involvement in the deaths of his wife and daughters. With Frederick senior himself and the Cotton boys who had died in West Auckland, we have difficult issues to face. No evidence regarding Frederick was found because the body was never recovered. There was no doubt that arsenic was found in the bodies of the Cotton boys and also that of Joseph Nattrass. The question to ask was how it got there. Mary Ann admitted that she may well have administered the arsenic, but insisted that it was not wilful or intentional and stated that she suspected that the arrowroot bought from Thomas Riley was contaminated. The residue found in her house apparently did not contain arsenic. We also know that Mary Ann used homeopathic mixtures and, as a nurse, may have administered these to the deceased. At that time there was no control over such things. Some practitioners did use arsenic as an ingredient. Was this the source of Mary Ann's comment about accidental poisoning? Did Smith's advice to say nothing cause her not to mention it?

Her lawyer at the trial raised the issue of arsenic being around the house in Front Street because of the arsenic soap. Scattergood had admitted that the soap could dry out and arsenic be made present. The defence could have done much more with this and brought in other expert opinion. Foster was hampered in this because of the short time between receiving the brief and the start of the trial. Then there was the use of arsenic-impregnated green wallpaper. It has been shown that neither the defence, nor Kilburn and Scattergood, appeared to have any knowledge of the controversy that was raging in Britain over this type of wallpaper. The defence, if they had had more time, may have discovered the necessary evidence of the Limehouse deaths and brought that to the attention of the court. It amazes me that Scattergood denied knowing of any deaths from this wallpaper. He was supposed to be a lecturer who was an expert on poisoning, yet this 'expert' was unaware of the Limehouse deaths and others, which had occurred many years previously. Research had also shown that the issues with the wallpaper did not always affect every person in a household. Despite the issue of green wallpaper already being a national scandal – it was even being raised in parliament – it was dismissed at the trial. We must question, as a matter of fairness, why available medical opinion was never raised at the trial. Even *The Lancet* queried this whole aspect of the case. It had been shown, on a number of occasions, that arsenic in a body may well have come from such wallpaper. Indeed Queen Victoria would later remove all green wallpaper from her houses because of the alarming proof of arsenic in these papers causing harm.

Finally, all the deaths occurred over a period when diseases of all sorts were endemic. Multiple deaths in families were a common experience. On the balance of probability, it would appear likely that these deaths were by poisoning. But, it is also possible that the deaths were caused by the presence of arsenic in an environment where those weakened by illness were more susceptible to its effects. It was argued that Mary Ann was the only one with both motive and opportunity, but this ignores the fact that the sum insured was relatively small. In the case of Nattrass for example, Mary Ann would have lost more financially from his death than she stood to gain.

Taking this fresh perspective on the evidence, the independent minded would surely accept that there is a reasonable doubt. When a case involves death as the only option for a guilty verdict, the jury must be 100 per cent certain of that guilt; if they are not, then another verdict must be considered. Mary Ann was also denied an appeal, which was a gross unfairness because an appeal may have produced new evidence relating to the green wallpaper.

So, was Mary Ann the West Auckland Borgia? My opinion is that she was not. It is to be remembered that she was only convicted of one murder. Although Mary Ann was remanded for the murders of Nattrass, Frederick junior and Robert Robson, all of whose bodies were exhumed, these cases were not heard in court and therefore the evidence was never tested. With Nattrass particularly, there was confusion with Dr Richardson's testimony. As for all the others, there is absolutely no shred of evidence produced to substantiate a case against her. I therefore do not believe that she is responsible for the number of murders attributed to her.

Was she guilty of any murders? I struggle to answer this question. It would be anachronistic to try and look at the situation with a modern mind. In that period, many things were black or white in legal terms. Information was not as easily accessible as it is in our internet age. Then, people did not have the knowledge and resources that we have in our police and legal system today. To judge her then is difficult. History has so blackened her name, she never gets a sympathetic hearing. I suppose I arrive at a place where I would bring in the Scottish legal judgement of 'Not Proven'. In other words, I don't know now, and I don't know what I would have decided then. I simply have a reasonable doubt and cannot offer the evidence with moral certainty. On the basis of pure evidence and on the conduct of her trial, I would argue that the guilty verdict should never have been reached.

Whatever the truth, there is a certainty: the body of Mary Ann Cotton is certainly rotten, but because of the allegations of poisonings, she will never be forgotten.

Schema of those associated with Mary Ann Cotton

Parents

Michael Robson	b.18212 d.1842
Margaret Lonsdale	b.1813 d.1867

Siblings

Margaret Robson	b.1834 d.1834
Robert Robson	b.1835 d.1860

Husbands

William Mowbray	b.1826 d.1865	
Mowbray Children		
	Cornwall Birth	b.1853? d?
	Cornwall Birth	b.1854? d?
	Cornwall Birth	b.1855? d?
	Margaret Jane	b.1856 d.1860
	Isabella	b.1858 d.1867
	Margaret Jane	b.1861 d.1865
	John Robert (William)	b.1863. d.1864
George Ward	b.1833 d.1866	
James Robinson	b.1833 d.1899	
Robinson Children		
(step) William Greenwell		b.1856
(step) Elizabeth		b.1859 d.1867
(step) James		b.1862 d.1867
(step) Mary Jane		b.1864
(step) John		b.1865 d.1866
	Margaret Isabella	b.1867 d.1868
	George	b.1869

Frederick Cotton (Bigamous Marriage)	b.1831 d.1871

Cotton Children

(step) Frederick junior	b.1862 d.1872
(step) Charles Edward	b.1865 d.1872
Robert Robson	b.1871 d. 1872

Frederick Cotton's Sister

Margaret Cotton   b.1832 d.1870

Lover

Joseph Nattrass   b.1836 d.1872

Margaret Edith

Quickmanning   b.1873 d.1954

(Possibly the daughter of Mary Ann and Joseph Nattrass)

Acknowledgements

All extracts of censuses, birth and death certificates, are © Crown Copyright and are used with permission of the Image Library, The National Archives, Kew, London.

Extracts from Parish Records have been used with permission.

The aerial photo of Johnson Terrace was given to the author and used with permission.

The photos of the Umbria, Cephalonia, William Calcraft and Thomas Dickson Archibald used here are understood to be out of copyright with no trace of the original owners being found. Anyone knowing otherwise please contact the author, to be credited in future editions.

Newspaper extracts are all from newspapers over 120 years old, and I would like to acknowledge *The Northern Echo* as a current newspaper, serving the North East for many years, reporting all the big stories, even at the time of Mary Ann Cotton.

The map of West Auckland 1857 and Townsend Chemist photo was kindly supplied by Mr John Niven, Architect at West Auckland, and used with his permission.

Thank you to Denise and Calum Ross for their assistance with the history of Brookfield Cottage and permission to use images of Thomas Riley's purchase of the cottage.

Dr Scattergood's image appears courtesy of 'University of Leeds Art Collection'.

Mr Charles Russell Q.C. Image dated: 5 May 1883 The original caption reads 'A Splendid Advocate' Published by *Vanity Fair* on that date. Printed by Vincent, Brook, Day & Sons. The artist has died and is unknown. Out of copyright and in the public domain.

Whorton, J.C., *The Arsenic Century: How Victorian Britain was poisoned at Home, Work and Play*. New York; Oxford University press, 2010

All other photographs used, and not credited within the text, are understood to be out of copyright or original and © copyright of the author.

Index